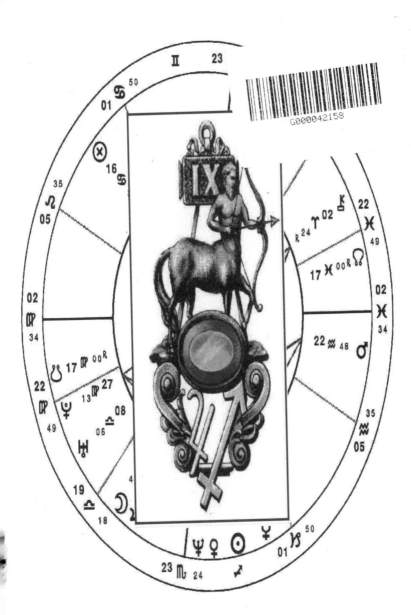

This book belongs to

....

of

....

and was presented on the occasion of

....

by...

on...

For Jo, Doug and Chloe

Astrology & Your Horse

Vicky and Beth Maloney

COMPASS EQUESTRIAN

HENLEY-IN-ARDEN

Line illustrations by Louise Heafield
Edited by Valerie Watson
Design: Alan Hamp

British Library Cataloguing in Publication Data
A catalogue record for this book is available from the
British Library

ISBN 1- 900667- 37-1

Published in Great Britain in 2000 by
Compass Equestrian Limited,
Cadborough Farm,
Oldberrow,
Henley-in-Arden,
Warwickshire, B95 5NX

© Vicky and Beth Maloney 2000

Printed in China
Produced by Phoenix Offset

CONTENTS

ACKNOWLEDGEMENTS

This book is dedicated to Harry, Nell and Nick with love.

Our sincere thanks also go to Valerie Watson and Barbara Cooper for having such enthusiasm for the idea and Felix, Blacks and Oscar who inspired the equestrian diversification !

The publishers wish to thank John Murray (publishers) Ltd for their permission to use the extract from John Betjamin's collected poems.
Extracts from Winnie the Pooh © A.A.Milne. Copyright under the Berne convention.Published by Methuen,an imprint of Egmont Children's books Ltd., London and used with permission.

SYNOPSIS OF SIGN QUALITIES

ARIES
Fire sign. Ruled by Mars. Compatible with other fire signs and with air signs.
Characteristics. Brave, independent, dynamic, competitive, headstrong.
Main body correspondence. Head and eyes.
Pertinent Herbs. Chamomile and thyme.
Tissue salts. Kali Phos. and Nat Phos.
Compatible colour. Red
Gemstone. Diamond
Suited to racing, cross country, polo and show jumping.

TAURUS
Earth sign. Ruled by Venus. Compatible with other earth signs and with water signs.
Characteristics. Solid, reliable, dependable, hard working, strong, stubborn and determined.
Main body correspondence. Throat and neck.
Pertinent herbs. Kelp and chicory.
Tissue salts: Nat Sulph. and Cal Sulph.
Compatible colours. Pale pink and light blue.
Gemstone. Sapphire
Suited to hard work trekking, hacking out, ploughing and agricultural work, riding school work or brood mare.

GEMINI
Air sign. Ruled by Mercury. Compatible with other air signs and with fire signs.
Characteristics. Quick, bright, intelligent, agile, versatile and adaptable.
Main body correspondence. Limbs and lungs.

Pertinent herbs. Lavender, nettle and garlic.
Tissue Salts. Calc Fluor. and Kali Mur.
Compatible colour. Yellow
Gemstone. Agate
Suited to show jumping, cross country, polo, point-to-pointing, and scurrying.

CANCER
Water sign. Ruled by the Moon. Compatible with other water signs and with the earth signs.
Characteristics. Sensitive, receptive, intuitive, caring, fluid and non-confrontational.
Main body correspondence. Udder, womb and stomach.
Pertinent herbs. Dried hops and chicory.
Tissue salts. Nux Vom. and Calc Phos.
Compatible colour. Silver
Gemstone: Pearl
Suited to riding school work, especially with disabled riders. An ideal brood mare or family pony.

LEO
Fire sign. Ruled by the Sun. Compatible with other fire signs and with air signs.

Characterisics. Proud, regal, noble, fun-loving, theatrical – a showman.
Main body correspondence. Heart and back.
Pertinent herbs. Dandelion and nettle
Tissue salts. Mag Phos. and Nat Mur.
Compatible colour. Gold.
Gemstones. Tiger eye and ruby.
Suited to dressage, showing, pageantry, theatre and circus.

VIRGO
Earth sign. Ruled by Mercury. Compatible with other earth signs and with water signs.
Characteristics. Intelligent, diligent, hardworking and productive.
Main body correspondence. Digestive system.
Pertinent herbs. Dill and garlic.
Tissue salts. Kali Sulph. and Ferri Phos.
Compatible colours. Dark indigo, green and brown.
Gemstones. Agate and sardonyx.
Suited to dressage, riding school work and ideal as a 'schoolmaster'.

LIBRA

Air sign. Ruled by Venus. Compatible with other air signs and with the fire signs.
Characteristics. Well mannered and intelligent, a companion and a strategist.
Main body correspondence. Kidneys and urinary tract.
Pertinent herbs. Thyme and parsley.
Tissue salts. Calc Phos. and Nat Phos.
Compatible colours. Pink and blue.
Gemstone. Sapphire
Suited to dressage, driving, side-saddle and any discipline which benefits from the use of strategy.

SCORPIO

Water sign. Ruled by Pluto and Mars. Compatible with other water signs and with earth signs.
Characteristics. Deep, intense, passionate, sensitive, determined, enduring and stubborn.
Main body correspondence. Sexual organs, rectum and bladder.
Pertinent herbs. Chicory, kelp and garlic.
Tissue salts: Calc Sulph. and Nat Sulph.
Compatible colour. Burgundy
Gemstone. Opal
Suited to long distance riding and cross country.

SAGITTARIUS

Fire sign. Ruled by Jupiter. Compatible with other fire signs and with air signs.
Characteristics. Generous, outgoing, adventurous, enthusiastic and willing. A risk taker.
Main body correspondence. Thighs and liver.
Pertinent herbs. Thyme and chicory.
Tissue salts. Silicia and Kali Mur.
Compatible colours. Royal blue and purple.
Gemstones. Turquoise and topaz.
Suited to long distance riding, cross country, hunting and show jumping.

CAPRICORN

Earth sign. Ruled by Saturn. Compatible with other earth signs and with water signs.
Characteristics. Sensitive, careful, cautious, predictable, diligent, hesitant, fearful but persistent.

Main body correspondence.
Skin, skeleton and knees.
Pertinent herbs. Comfrey and
calendula.
Tissue salts. Calc Phos. and
Calc Fluor.
Compatible colour. Black
Gemstone. Jet.
Suited to any discipline
which is structured and
which requires persistent
effort.

AQUARIUS
Air sign. Ruled by Uranus
and Saturn. Compatible
with other air signs and
with the fire signs.
Characteristics. Enigmatic,
mentally agile, intelligent,
unpredictable, stubborn and
rebellious.
Main body correspondence.
Circulatory system.
Pertinent herbs. Rosemary
and nettle.
Tissue salts. Nat Mur. and
Mag Phos.
Compatible colour. Electric
blue.

Gemstone. Amethyst.
Suited to racing and show
jumping.

PISCES
Water sign. Ruled by
Neptune and Jupiter.
Compatible with other
water signs and with the
earth signs.
Characteristics. Intuitive,
imaginative, gentle,
malleable, impressionable,
and receptive.
Main body correspondence.
Lymphatic system, hooves,
duodenum.
Pertinent herbs. Kelp and
nettle.
Compatible colour. Sea green.
Gemstone. Moonstone.
Suited to dressage (in
particular dressage to music),
trekking and to riding
school work.

SIGNS OF THE ZODIAC

Sign Name	Symbol (Glyph)	Dates[1]	Element[2]	Planetary Ruler	
Aries	♈	21 March–20 April	Fire	Mars	♂
Taurus	♉	20 April–21 May	Earth	Venus	♀
Gemini	♊	21 May–22 June	Air	Mercury	☿
Cancer	♋	22 June–23 July	Water	Moon	☽
Leo	♌	23 July–23 Aug.	Fire	Sun	☉
Virgo	♍	23 Aug.–22 Sept.	Earth	Mercury	☿

Sign Name	Symbol (Glyph)	Dates[1]	Element[2]	Planetary Ruler
Libra	♎	22 Sept.–24 Oct.	Air	Venus ☿
Scorpio	♏	24 Oct.–23 Nov.	Water	Pluto ♇
Sagittarius	♐	23 Nov.–22 Dec.	Fire	Jupiter ♃
Capricorn	♑	22 Dec.–21 Jan.	Earth	Saturn ♄
Aquarius	♒	21 Jan.–20 Feb.	Air	Uranus ♅
Pisces	♓	20 Feb.–21 Mar.	Water	Neptune ♆

1. These dates are only a guide and will occasionally vary by one or two days. For an accurate date consult an ephemeris, the tables on page 109 or an astrologer.
2. As a general rule, Fire is compatible with Air and Earth is compatible with Water.

INTRODUCTION

Whatever is born or done this moment has the
qualities of this moment of time.
The Secret of The Golden Flower. C.G. Jung.

SINCE 800 BC and the ancient Mesopotamians, man has looked up to the heavens for guidance. The sky was then as it is now, the source of many weird and wonderful phenomena for which he sought explanations.

Each day the Sun appeared on the eastern horizon at dawn, to journey towards its zenith and make its descent towards the western horizon, setting each evening at dusk. But its time of arrival and departure varied slightly from one dawn to the next, increasing or decreasing the daylight hours in sequence. These variations were observed and recorded but were not understood.

Early man had no way of knowing that having set, the Sun would reappear. This troubled him because he knew that without the Sun's life-giving rays, food would not grow and life as he knew it would not exist. The Sun possessed special powers of light and warmth on which he depended for his survival. These powers were seen to be divine. The Sun was deified and was worshiped as a god. Prayers were said to him in thanks for his arrival at dawn and were again offered at dusk for his safe passage through the darkness of the night. This was a masculine god because he was seen to be the giver of life.

The next most visible body in the sky was the Moon. From out of the darkness of a moonless night sky would appear a thin sliver of light which, as the nights passed grew in size and shape to become a fully formed bright disc of light. It would then begin to fade until eventually it was no more. This night light was thought to be the Sun's wife or consort. She appeared fresh and new, became pregnant and round, gave birth to her progeny withered into old age and died. She was the maid, the mother and the old crone. Eventually, the connection was made between her 28 day cycle and the female menstrual cycle. This lunar goddess was worshiped as the female receptive energy of gestation and birth. She was thought to be the sustainer of life.

The Sun and the Moon were part of man's natural environment. That his survival was dependent upon them formed the basis of religion. It was not until several centuries later that the understanding of its gravitational pull provided evidence of the Moon controlling the ebb and flow of the tides.

The stars, believed then to be the progeny of the Moon, were also thought to be divine. Against the backdrop of a clear night sky, certain stars were seen to move along the same path as the Sun and the Moon. These stars, now known to be planets, were then called wanderers. They were thought to be the messengers of the Sun and the Moon. Their appearance and disappearance was seen to correlate with events that took place on Earth. For instance the appearance of the morning and evening star, rising and setting with the Sun coincided with times of peace and harmony, tranquillity and beauty. These gods and goddesses were also given names that described the influence they had upon earthly events.

Pictorial records were kept of all this strange celestial activity. From the long and detailed observations of the wise men of the time (the original astrologers), maps of the sky were made. The path around the Earth which the Sun, Moon and planets appeared to take, was divided into twelve equal sections. Each section was named after the constellation of stars that fell within it at the time. The constellations were themselves named after familiar things on Earth; things that were held in awe by man because they possessed extraordinary powers. When a planet appeared in a particular section of the path around the Earth, its influence was execised by qualities of that particular sign. The path is what we call the Zodiac.

The earliest known pictorial representation of the Zodiac is on the ceiling of the Temple of Hathor at Denderah in Egypt. It dates from around 100 BC, although the original, taken to Paris in the 19th century, is thought to be many thousands of years older.

This ancient Zodiac clearly depicts the animals that symbolise the various signs. The Ram shows off the quick, headstrong and independent characteristics of Aries; the Bull indicates the slower, steadier qualities of Taurus, whilst the Lion illustrates the proud and regal qualities for which the sign of Leo is renowned.

In a language understood globally, these visual images convey the qualities innate in each of the twelve signs. The ancient Greeks developed them further, to become the Zodiac we use today.

Early Astrology was concerned only with omens. Man did not consider things to be accidental. He believed that everything was ordained by some greater power, and that everything had a meaning. Anything which appeared to defy explanation, he attributed to a physical source. This gave him a feeling of security. Today those of us who read the stars in the daily newspapers or in our favourite magazines are doing much the same thing.

It was not until the end of the 19th and beginning of the 20th centuries that astrology began to be used as a tool for self awareness and self development. Only then did astrologers begin to recognise its psychological value.

Today we are able to use the horoscope as a map of the psyche, from which we can assess the character and the potential of its owner, whether human or animal.

The word horoscope is from two Greek words, 'hora', the hour, and 'skopos', to observe. The essence of people and creatures, their emotional needs and responses, the way in which they think and relate, their goals, ambitions, aspirations, fears, uncertainties and inadequacies, can all be determined from a natal horoscope. The value of this is obvious in human terms. It is equally valuable when it is used for someone who is unable to communicate his or her feelings and needs. Our desire to communicate with animals has been well illustrated through the popularity of literary works, from 'The Jungle Book' and 'Doctor Doolittle' to the novel, 'The Horse Whisperer' whose plot is worked around the ancient skill of being able to understand what a horse needs or is trying to communicate by reading its body language.

Monty Roberts has more than adequately demonstrated through his work how understanding the psychological make up of the horse, facilitates easier, kinder and more humane handling. His insight enables him to quickly solve problems that would otherwise remain unsolved.

In this book we show how astrology can be used to give an accurate insight into the psychological makeup of horses. With the information provided, owners will understand their charges better and be able to provide an environment and life style to which their individual horses are most naturally suited.

From earliest times through the study of astrology, man has understood intuitively what Carl Jung, philosopher, recognised and documented. That is, whatever is done at a moment of time, embodies the qualities of that moment of time. Anyone or anything born during the time span of a Zodiac sign, embodies the characteristics of that sign.

CHAPTER 1

SUN SIGN, MOON SIGN.

The Signs Of The Zodiac.

Now constellations Muse and signs rehearse,
In order let them sparkle in thy verse;
First Aries, glorious in his golden wool,
Looks back, and wonders at the mighty Bull,
Whose hind parts first appear, he bending lies
With threatening head and calls the Twins to rise;
They clasp for fear, and mutually embrace,
And next the Twins with an unsteady pace
Bright Cancer tolls, then Leo shakes his mane
And following Virgo calms his rage again.
Then day and night are weighed in Libra's scales
Equal awhile, at last the night prevails;
And longer grown the heavier scale inclines
And draws bright Scorpio from the winter signs,
Him Centaur follows with an aiming eye,
His bow full drawn and ready to let fly,
Next narrow horns, the wisted Caper shows,
And from Aquarius urn a flood o'erflows.
Near their lov'd waves cold Pisces take their seat,
With Aries join and make the round complete.

Marcus Manillius. Greece. C0.A.D.

THE SIGN that is said to rule the horse is the sign of Sagittarius. It is symbolised by a Centaur, half man, half horse. Most Sagittarians have a love of horses and many people who live or work with horses have this sign emphasised in their own personalities.

When we refer to the Sun sign we are talking about what most people know as their star sign. This is the sign of the zodiac in which the Sun falls at any given time of the year. Just as the Sun is the centre of our solar system, so the Sun in the horoscope refers to the core or central being. It describes the qualities of the life giving force, the vital spirit and the individuality.

For example if your horse or pony is born in the Northern Hemisphere between 20 March and 19 April he will have the Sun in Aries. The qualities of the sign of Aries will therefore govern his essence and how he expresses himself. Essentially independent, brave and headstrong, this animal is a natural leader. He will be most at ease in an environment where he knows he is the boss and where he has a team to follow him.

The sign in which the Moon was placed when he was born will also have a strong influence upon his character. It will determine his moods, responses and reactions. It will also say something about his caring and protective nature. For instance, if your horse or pony was born with the Moon rather than the Sun in the sign of Aries, his reactions would be governed by the qualities of Aries. He would therefore be impulsive and impatient in his response to things. Keen to get on with whatever has to be done, he will feel cross and bad tempered if he has to wait around for too long.

The Sun takes one year to complete its round of the Zodiac. It remains within each sign for one month entering the first sign, Aries, on the Vernal, or spring, Equinox.

The Moon takes twenty-eight days to circle the Zodiac, spending approximately two and a half days in each sign. You can find out where the Sun and the Moon were on the day when your horse or pony was born, by consulting the tables at the end of the book. If your horse or pony was born abroad, you will need to make the necessary adjustment from local time and date to GMT time and date before using the tables.

To blend together your horse's Sun sign and Moon sign you need to remember that the characteristics described in the following chapters apply to his essential character if they refer to his Sun sign. These same characteristics will influence his response, reactions, moods and emotional behaviour if they relate to his Moon sign. He will display his Sun characteristics when he is expressing himself, his Moon characteristics when his emotions are triggered. He will sometimes show both. The examples we use later in the book illustrate how this works. Ideally his lifestyle and environment should accommodate his solar behaviour, in order for him to thrive, and his lunar needs in order for him to feel secure.

To find your horse's Sun sign and Moon sign refer to Appendices 1 and 2 at the end of the book.

Most foals are born during the early hours of the morning. In their natural state and without human intervention mares generally begin to foal in late spring and foaling continues throughout the summer. This gives the newborn animals the benefit of the better grass, longer daylight hours and finer weather.

However, for reasons of convenience and economy we intervene in this natural process. The outcome of our intervention is that in the Northern Hemisphere, Thoroughbreds are born as near as possible to January 1st each year. The breeding season for Non-Thoroughbreds, while closer to the natural pattern, has been extended, to begin in very early spring and continues until the autumn.

Consequently, in the Northern Hemisphere, Thoroughbred horses will be born with the Sun in Capricorn, or possibly Aquarius if the foaling is late. Other foals are likely to be born between the signs of Pisces and Libra. By Scorpio, the days are getting shorter and the life force is turned inward. The grass stops growing and what remains has very little nutritional value. Foals born in this hemisphere after that time would need a lot of extra care to ensure their survival.

CHAPTER 2

THE FIRE SIGNS

THE THREE FIRE SIGNS are Aries, Leo and Sagittarius. All three are very volatile. All three observe the possibilities innate in any given situation. This gives them a spirit of adventure and a strong desire to create something from all those possibilities. Their vision, intuition and insight manifests as hunches which they follow unquestioningly, usually to their advantage.

* Aries is the cardinal fire sign. It initiates action.
* Leo is the fixed fire sign. It consolidates action.
* Sagittarius is the mutable fire sign. It moves the action on, so that it becomes something more.

The fire signs are direct and uncomplicated. They have tremendous strength and enthusiasm as well as faith in themselves. In order to express their high energy they need to be given plenty of space and freedom. Childlike in their simplicity they do not understand subtle nuances. Their enthusiasm can make them act in haste. Their impatience, strong will and their lack of self-control can create problems for them and their riders.

ARIES

... "Not I' said the duck,
'Not I' said the dog,
'Not I' said the cat,
Then I'll do it myself' said the Little Red Hen.
And she did!"
> *The Little Red Hen & The Grain of Wheat.*
> Joseph Jacobs.

The quotation from the children's story, 'The Little Red Hen', aptly describes the independence of the Aries temperament. Faced with something that needs to be done the Aries character will rise to the occasion.

Aries is a cardinal fire sign. That is to say, it is one which is active, outgoing and initiating. Ruled by the warrior planet Mars, it bestows upon your horse the spirit of adventure. In days of old, the ideal war horse, brave in battle would have been an Aries; the perfect partner for Crusaders or Knights rushing off to rescue damsels in distress, 'charge' is the battle cry to which the Aries horse will most willingly respond – often before the cry has been given. His modern day equivalent is perhaps a horse of the Royal Horse Artillery King's Troop.

The Aries horse's spirit of adventure is strong and he will be at his best when he has a challenge to rise to. Brave and independent his temperament is suited to any kind of work that requires courage. He will be happy living and working with other horses, but it is worth re-iterating that if he is to be part of a team, you will get the best results

calendula ~ euphrasia ~

~chamomile~nettle~thyme~kali.phos

thyme~kali.phos

chamomile~nettle~

calendula ~ euphrasia

from him if he is given the position of leader. Otherwise, you could just find him trying to follow from the front

as the quote from Winnie the Pooh suggests, ... *'he was the sort of Tigger who was always in front when you were showing him the way'* .

The Aries horse's desire to get on with things may well manifest as rash or impulsive behaviour. On the flat or over fences he is likely to lead the field. Out hunting you and he could come a cropper if, in his desire to be first home, he leaps before he looks. Because he will want to do everything as quickly as possible, given his head, the Aries horse should be able to find the short cuts. However, your courage had better be a match for his if you are to cope with the terrain he may take you through in order to get home ahead of everyone else.

His competitive streak and his natural enthusiasm make him an ideal competition horse. He has a good brain that will be keen to try out new ways of doing things. But beware his tendency to act in haste, lest you both repent at leisure.

A sedentary lifestyle will not suit this dynamic and out-going creature at all well. Given little to do and insufficient exercise he is likely to become restless, even aggressive. Without an appropriate outlet for his high energy he may become jumpy, spooking at anything and everything.

The disciplines to which you will find your Aries horse most likely to be suited are racing, either flat or over fences, cross country and show jumping. His bravery and his speed should make the Aries pony ideal for polo, but as an eventer, dressage could well be the stumbling block for both horses and ponies. They lack the patience required for such a precise discipline and they will not like to be controlled in this manner. Their Aries temperament wants to take the initiative. This makes following tests difficult for them. They are much happier inventing their own, which can often result in you riding one test while your Aries steed rides another. If you try to make him do otherwise a full-blown tantrum in front of everyone is likely to be the only result you achieve.

When it comes to schooling and training it is important not to set up situations which will require a battle. Remember the Aries needs to win at all costs. Methods which are both challenging and fun but which do not create rivalry between you and him are likely to be the most successful.

It is perhaps already apparent to you that your Aries companion will be most content in an environment where he can be turned out and allowed plenty of natural exercise. If this is not possible and he does have to be stabled, a busy yard where there is plenty going on will probably suit him better than somewhere where he will easily get bored. Stable vices such as weaving, cribbing and windsucking are signs of boredom to look out for.

An Aries pony needs a plucky and competent rider. He is not likely to be the best buy for an absolute novice or for a child who can only ride at weekends. Hacking him out alone could be risky, as he might decide to charge off, or to do battle with a passing motorist. Remember the Aries words, headstrong, headfirst, headache. If you find yourself the owner of an Aries horse or pony with which you are not a good match, you could find all three a part of your daily life.

Adults and children be aware: here is an animal who requires time, energy and enthusiasm. If you have these and have gained a good level of competence and confidence; are able to hack out with someone else and ride off the roads; if you share his competitive spirit and/or you enjoy a challenge, the Aries horse is one for you to look out for.

All three fire signs are blessed with abundant energy and vitality. The down side of this is that they can use their energy recklessly. This sometimes leads to ill health and accidents. Physical symptoms of Aries' disease are fevers and inflammations. His bolshy behaviour towards you is also a typical trait. His enthusiasm for work will allow you to keep him busy all the time, but ideally he should balance work with relaxation. Periods of relaxation, in an environment that gives him room to move around and things to keep him occupied, will do much to restore his energy after bouts of hard work.

Any ailment which stops your Aries horse being able to get on with his life will be a source of great irritation to him. This again will be made clear to you via his bad tempered behaviour. However, his courage will enable him to meet any serious disability bravely and he is unlikely ever to bear a grudge.

Aries horses respond particularly well to Acupuncture and massage. The massage soothes the wear and tear on tired muscles, and acupuncture will release blocked energy channels and generally restore balance.

Calendula cream and Arnica are useful first aid standbys. Both assist with healing cuts and abrasions, while Euphrasia works like magic on inflamed or weepy eyes; something to which you could find your Aries horse is particularly vulnerable.

The herbs from which he should benefit are comfrey, chamomile, nettle and thyme. These are easy to add to his feed in either their fresh or dried forms. The tissue salt for the Aries nature is Potassium Phosphate which is naturally present in dandelions.

Impatiens is the Bach flower remedy associated with the sign of Aries. A few drops in your Aries horse's water bucket each day should work wonders on his impatient and impulsive temperament.

LEO

'If any body wants to clap, now is the time to do it'
Winnie the Pooh. A. A. Milne.

When the sign of Leo is emphasised in the character of your horse or pony it is important that you are prepared to become his willing and appreciative audience. With this element as the essence of his being, your Leo horse or pony will require constant praise and attention in order to satisfy his strong need for recognition. In return he will give you enduring affection and loyalty.

The Lion is the symbol for the sign of Leo. This describes the regal and noble characteristics innate within your horse. He is naturally proud and will not want to behave in a manner that will bring shame or disgrace upon him or you. However, should you ignore him or fail to acknowledge his achievements he will play up or show off in order to gain the attention he craves.

hyssop ~ borage ~ nettle ~ rosemary ~ dandelion ~ angelica ~ rosemary ~ nettle ~ borage ~ hyssop ~ dandelion ~ angelica

Whether a horse or a pony, this animal is a foal at heart. His love of play is an endearing characteristic which needs to be recognised and honoured. This is not an animal who will cope well with routine and drudgery. He needs to have fun. His work should therefore provide him with this fun. His endeavours should be rewarded with the recognition and applause he desires.

Leo is the sign of fixed fire. Aries, the first fire sign has the quality of the initial spark which gets things going, but it lacks perseverance. Leo is the second fire sign. Its fixed and permanent quality adds endurance. This enables your Leo horse or pony to overcome obstacles and to persevere in the face of adversity. On the down side it makes him stubborn. Once he has decided upon a course of action it will take a great deal to persuade him otherwise. A playful distraction is likely to work better than force.

The Leo horse is a natural show horse; pageantry and ceremony suit him well because he wants to be in the limelight. He believes his rightful place is centre stage and the louder the applause the better he likes it. Failure from his 'audience' to respond to his efforts will make him downcast and unsure of himself. Your enthusiasm and involvement in his activities will make him feel highly prized. Your appreciation will reaffirm for him his sense of being special. On this he thrives. The Leo horse will put his heart into everything he does. His desire to be best is matched only by his desire to have the best. He is the king of his own particular stable yard and as such will want to be given treatment befitting his regal status. Why should he settle for second best when he can have the best? After all he gives you his best. He expects you to return the compliment. When you do he will respond with love and devotion.

Because Leo horses are so young at heart they are often

good with children, being naturally in tune with them. They will enjoy the attention given by children . If you put a Leo pony with a young rider who, like him, enjoys dressing up and showing off her skills, you are sure to have a winning team.

Although essentially robust, should too much be heaped upon this worthy steed, he will not be able to bear it. Your Leo horse could then turn into a very difficult and demanding creature who will throw tantrums or behave in a very unpleasant, attention seeking fashion. Such behaviour in a show jumping arena or in the middle of a cross-country course could have disastrous results for you both.

The Leo horse's response to anything which makes him feel insecure will be a theatrical one. And you can be sure his timing will be impeccable. What better place than the water jump to ditch an unappreciative rider ? Sir John Betjeman's poem *'Hunter Trials'* clearly illustrates the Leo pony

> *'Oh wasn't it naughty of Smudges?*
> *Oh, Mummy, I'm sick with disgust.*
> *She threw me in front of the Judges,*
> *And my silly old collarbone's bust'*

Your Leo pony's pride becomes your fall. Better to recognise his limits and ensure that he is only ever in a situation where you know he will be able to shine.

Obviously any showing class should be perfect for him – as should be dressage. Here he can display his organisational skills and his powers of concentration, while at the same time showing off how beautifully he moves. The glamour and drama of the circus should appeal to the theatrical side of his nature, so long as he is well cared for. And who could be better to take a role in films, advertising or theatre? The ponies chosen for the ballet *'La Fille Mal Garde'* or the *'Cinderella'* pantomime must surely be Leo ponies!

Because your Leo, along with his other fiery friends, is inclined to overestimate how much he can do, he is susceptible to overload. He wants to do everything you ask of him. His back will be one of the first places to register any stress. You should also keep an eye out for heart problems. Equine influenza and other viruses, if not treated properly can lead to irregular heartbeat, arrythmia and myocarditis, which in extreme cases can result in heart failure. Once contracted myocarditis requires prolonged rest.

Given the right treatment for any ailment the Leo temperament will endure such difficulties with courage and fortitude. Plenty of gentle, balanced exercise is obviously helpful in avoiding heart disorders. It also helps to maintain a supple back. Gentle manipulation should bring about improvement if problems do occur, although there is some dispute amongst horse owners as to whether osteopathy actually works as an effective treatment for horses.

Nux Vomica is the homeopathic remedy recommended for Leos suffering from strain. Muscle strain responds well to Rhus Tox. Aconitum 30 is helpful for palpitations caused by tension. All three can be administered in tablet form either directly into the mouth or mixed with the feed. You will need to speak to a professional homeopath to formulate the correct dose for your horse.

Dandelion, as its name suggests, is the herb of Leo. Nettle is also very beneficial. Both are easily available, growing naturally in fields and pastures which have not been treated with weed killers. Both purify the blood and act as a tonic especially beneficial for Leo types. Other herbs with a similar effect are angelica, borage, hyssop and rosemary, while mustard can be helpful for alleviating back pains. All of these can be added to the feed.

The Bach flower remedy Vervain can be helpful for exhaustion when your Leo horse has been taking on too much or trying too hard. It also reduces stubbornness. Vervain needs only to be used in very small amounts and can be added to the drinking water.

A Leo pony should make the perfect children's pony. Given a home where he is loved and given plenty of attention he should thrive. In any environment where he is made to feel special and where he doesn't have to compete for attention, your Leo horse should do well, responding to your affection with warmth and loyalty.

SAGITTARIUS

'the road of excess leads to the palace of wisdom'
William Blake.

The third and last fire sign of the zodiac is Sagittarius, whose symbol is that of the Archer and Centaur. Sagittarius is the sign most associated with horses. The Centaur illustrates the strong link between the horse and people born under this sign. Most people born during the sign of Sagittarius love horses and many of them are involved with horses either professionally or as a hobby.

In the northern hemisphere, the shorter days and colder weather from mid-November to mid-December are not ideal for foaling or for rearing young foals. Unless your horse or pony was born in the southern hemisphere, it is unlikely that he will have been born when the Sun was in the sign of Sagittarius. However if he was, you will be the proud owner of a generous and willing steed. The Moon is in Sagittarius for approximately two and a half days every month, so a horse or pony with the Moon in Sagittarius is a much more likely prospect. His Sagittarius characteristics will be apparent in the way he responds to given situations. They also describe what he needs in order to feel secure. To find out when the Moon is in the sign of Sagittarius, look at Appendix 2 at the rear of the book.

In days of old when the horse was the only alternative to Shank's pony for getting from A to B, a Sagittarius horse would have made the perfect travelling companion. The sign of Sagittarius rules long distance travel. It also rules

bay ~ borage ~ thyme ~
chicory ~ dandelion ~ rosemary
thyme ~ borage ~ bay ~ chicory ~ dandelion ~ rosemary

foreign countries. Since time immemorial the Sagittarius horse has been used to carry the heroes of history across continents, enabling them to increase their territories and expand their horizons.

Sagittarius horse is highly intelligent, full of natural exuberance and is happy to give. His desire to extend the realm of his own experience motivates him to rise to each challenge you put before him with courage and enthusiasm. But as with the other two fire signs, Aries and Leo, your Sagittarius horse will be inclined to take on more than he can easily cope with. For the Sagittarius spirit, 'too much' is definitely better than 'enough'.

The fire of Sagittarius is as forest fire. It is active and changeable. It travels far and fast. Your Sagittarius horse or pony will do the same. His spirit of adventure will stimulate him to go further and further. He is not afraid to take risks and will not allow obstacles to stand in his way. More probably he will clear them without a second thought. He will therefore need a competent rider (with good breaks). Should he get the ' bit between his teeth' without someone and something to hold him back, there will be no stopping him.

The Sagittarius horse's need to cover as much ground as possible makes him ideally suited for long distance riding. He is less well suited to detailed work as he tends to overlook the details in favour of the bigger picture. His eye is on the distant horizon. This is obviously a disadvantage for dressage, but he should do well over fences, or at show jumping as long as his rider knows the course. Out hunting and across-country and he will strive to lead the field.

His desire to go further and further will apply to whatever he does. Keeping the Sagittarius horse focussed on the current situation will require a degree of skill and understanding. Before he has finished the job in hand he will be looking for what comes next. This coupled with his naturally generous spirit,(which wants to give you all you ask of him), will make it extremely easy to overstretch him. Once your Sagittaruis horse is engaged in something that interests him, his vision of what is possible will be endless. Should you share this same breadth of vision there should be no stopping you. Establishing a sensible exercise regime and sticking to it will benefit him and you. It will help you both to avoid burn out.

It is perhaps already apparent that a Sagittarius horse or pony is not a novice ride. He needs a rider who is a match for his adventurous spirit and his great courage. However, his rider also needs to recognise both their limits. Should they overestimate their capabilities they, like the Greek hero Bellerophon on his winged horse Pegasus, could well find themselves tumbling to earth with a very resounding crash.

Essentially good natured, very little will crush the spirit of your Sagittarius horse or pony for long. Deflated for a while, he will soon get over setbacks and will be ready to face every new challenge with optimism and enthusiasm.

A single factor which will cause your Sagittarius horse the greatest of stress is restriction. He needs space – and lots of it. Also, ideally he needs the companionship of other horses. He is not an animal who will cope well with being stabled all the time. Nor will he cope with a regime where he is only let out to graze for an hour or two every day. Sagittarius horse needs to be turned out in a field or big paddock and it suits him best to live out all the time. Buy him a good rug or two and if possible give him the space he needs. Similarly if you are travelling a Sagittarius horse, make sure he has plenty of room to move. When you box him, ensure that he can see his way out, otherwise getting him into such a confined space could be a real headache.

If your horse has to be stabled, limit it to as short a time as you can and balance it with plenty of outdoor exercise. If his needs are not met he will be inclined to procrastinate. Restlessness and irritability will be the inevitable result of a lifestyle which is too restricting or confined. A Sagittarius pony is a little Houdini. He doesn't like being fenced in and he will tell you so. Be sure your fences are really stock proof.

Should your Sagittarius horse or pony overdo things, it is likely to be his hind-quarters that let him down first. While he is fit and strong his hind-quarters will remain powerful. When his lifestyle is too sedentary problems may well arise.

Sagittarius horses' livers are quite vulnerable to excess. Remember, for them, 'too much' is better than 'enough'. They will not be able to discriminate when food is too rich for them. If you give a Sagittarius horse access to unlimited food, he won't know when he has had enough. Ad lib grazing on an abundance of rich pasture is therefore best avoided. This is the horse or pony who will even gorge himself on ragwort if it is available to him, resulting in the extremely undesirable ragwort poisoning, which can in turn lead to hepatitis - a good reason to check your fields regularly no matter what sign your horse is born under.

Greedy Sagittarius ponies are more than usually susceptible to laminitis. This in itself is a painful and distressing ailment. Should you then starve your pony in an attempt to cure him of the laminitis you could cause hyperlipaemia which can be fatal. Watching your pony's diet is therefore essential to his well being. A structured diet that gives your horse or pony the food value he needs in order to do the work expected of him, without putting stress on his liver, is clearly well worth the effort. The homeopathic remedy Nux Vomica 6 is useful for liver upsets. Rhus Tox 6 helps alleviate muscle strain. Chicory is known to have a beneficial effect upon the liver.

Herbs which benefit the Sagittarius makeup are bay, borage, dandelion, rosemary and chicory. All are useful for liver conditions. Thyme is cleansing and antiseptic as well as a good liver tonic. These remedies can be added to the feed.

CHAPTER 3

THE EARTH SIGNS

THE THREE EARTH SIGNS are Taurus, Virgo and Capricorn. All three are concerned with the tangible and material world of here and now. They are all practical, solid and dependable and all three experience life through the senses. Security and safety is important to them all.

* Taurus is the fixed earth sign. It is the most reliable, stubborn and resistant to change.
* Virgo is the mutable earth sign. It is the most flexible, the most able to adapt to changing conditions.
* Capricorn is the cardinal earth sign. It initiates organised and structured activity.

The Earth signs understand how the material world functions, but their outlook is a narrow one. They are not risk takers, they prefer to stick with what they know. In tune with the world of form, they know instinctively how to get their most basic needs met. Their passive and persistent nature does not give up or give in. They are able to endure much more than the other signs and once they set themselves a goal they will keep going until they have achieved it. Resistant to any form of change their stubborn refusal to give up can lead to their downfall. These Earthy creatures respond well to the sensitivity of the water signs, Cancer, Scorpio and Pisces whose gentle persuasion can soften even the most rigid determination.

TAURUS

'Always good tempered, always pleased to see you, always sorry when you go... So simple, so good natured and so affectionate.'
      The Wind In The Willows. Kenneth Grahame.

As the quotation from *The Wind in the Willow* suggests, the Taurus temperament is uncomplicated, and straightforward.

Taurus is the first of the three Earth signs. Its fixity makes your Taurus horse or pony very stubborn and strong willed. This is an animal who thrives on routine and who will firmly resist any kind of change, to his timetable or environment. He likes things to remain the same. Happiest with all that is known, tried and tested, Taurus horse will want to be fed and turned out at the same time each day, have his feed in the same bucket, in the same part of the field(or stable) and be given regular exercise, regularly. Whilst not the ideal temperament of horse for an owner who leads an unpredictable or erratic lifestyle, he is instead, the perfect companion for anyone who enjoys an orderly existence. An affectionate good nature makes the Taurus mare an excellent mother. The practical and protective qualities she possesses should make bonding with her foals

~sage~ nat sulp

~vervain~kelp

chicory~

~chicory~kelp~vervain~

nat. sulp~sage~

problem free. Separation could prove more difficult. She is inclined to be quite possessive of her young and will probably fret if they are taken from her before she is ready to let them go.

Because Taurus horses experience life via their senses, they need to feel that they are in a comfortable environment in order to feel safe and secure. Warmth, affection and constancy are as necessary to their sense of well being, as are a permanent shelter and sufficient food. Given a lifestyle that offers stability, they will gain trust and confidence, becoming loyal and dependable friends.

All horses use their senses in order to evaluate what is happening around them. Your Taurus horse or pony will have a particularly well developed sense of smell. This is not only helpful to the Taurus mare in recognising her foals, it also makes her more than usually sensitive to her environment. It enables her to pick up on fear or danger instantly, even when the cause is still a long way off. A wise owner would do well to take heed of her signals, rather than disregarding them or brushing them off as an over reaction. This same well developed sense will tell the Taurus stallion when the mares are in season before his fellow stallions pick up on it.

Happy to be turned out in a familiar field where there is plenty of good grazing, Taurus horses will be content to be left to their own devices. In fact one of the downsides to their personalities is the inclination to become lazy and over weight. Perfectly content to be fed, groomed and put to bed each night, they need encouragement to work. Otherwise a naturally relaxed attitude could very easily turn into apathy.

The Taurus horse does not like to be pushed or rushed. He prefers to do things in his own way and at his own pace. If you have very set ideas about what you want from him, you will need to be patient. He will respond best to a programme of exercise that gradually builds up to whatever you have in mind for him. Start slowly and introduce things one at a time. Give him the opportunity to get used to each new challenge before asking more of him. It may seem to take forever but the endurance of a Taurus horse is second to none. He will persevere with even the most arduous tasks, determined to overcome obstacles that would defeat more fickle temperaments. Handle him properly and you will find you are well rewarded for your time and patience. Reward him with a tasty morsel and your Taurus horse will be putty in your hands.

Not easily spooked or flustered this steady and reliable steed is an ideal children's pony or novice ride. He may not gain red rosettes for cross-country and he isn't likely to make you a fortune at the race-course but handled properly, he is safe and reliable; a must if you want to take him out on the roads.

Usually quite solidly built, with a strong neck and shoulders, Taurus horses are built to work. Unless her Moon sign suggests otherwise, the Taurus mare is not designed for speed, but built for endurance. Although she lacks agility (and can sometimes be quite clumsy), strong feet and limbs, well sprung ribs and a wide pelvis make her a perfect brood mare. Heavy plough horses such as Shire horses are excellent examples of the Taurus physique. Their solidity and their love of nature ideally equips them for work in the fields. Their need to see concrete evidence of their efforts is rarely better satisfied than when they leave a well ploughed field at the end of a hard days work.

Similarly your Taurus horse or pony will be revitalised when he is at one with nature. He draws much of his energy from the earth. It quite literally nourishes and sustains him. It follows therefore that Taurus horses are not likely to be happy if they are shut in all the time. If you are able to hack your Taurus horse out, the beauty of the countryside will calm and soothe him. He is in tune with its cycles.

The ideal trekking pony, Taurus pony will relish taking the same path day after day. His protective nature will take pride in ensuring who ever he carries feels safe with him. His great tolerance should enable him to cope with any lack of experience on the part of his riders and who better to get them home safely at the end of their trek?

Constitutionally very strong, if Taurus horse is well cared for he should enjoy robust good health. However, his surroundings are important to his well being and too little exercise or a poor diet will both take their toll. Change will also affect him adversely, so is best avoided whenever possible.

Subjected to a lifestyle that doesn't suit him, your Taurus horse or pony could loose interest in his surroundings and in his work. He will then become dull and depressed. Weight gain from fluid retention is possible so you should keep an eye open for filled legs. He is also likely to be susceptible to inflamed or infected sinuses, to retention of mucus or to a runny nose from hay-fever. Any tension in his neck and shoulders should respond well to massage, which he will love even if it is given just as a treat. Taurus mare's sensitivity to touch is as pronounced as her sense of smell, so that even stroking her for a minute or two each time you see her will soothe her and make her feel loved.

This same sensitivity combined with a naturally placid nature makes the Taurus horse good for side saddle riding, as he will immediately register the slightest movement of hand and leg. Put this together with a love of routine, repetition and familiarity and you should also have the perfect dressage horse or pony, especially when the dressage is to music.

Along with his appreciation of comfort and routine Taurus horse has a tremendous love of food. Although he is fond of rich and sweet things, he is better suited to a natural diet that is not too rich- one that is high in fibre with carefully measured amounts of protein should suit him best. Taking the trouble to sort out the diet that is right for him will pay dividends in the end.

If you find that stubbornness is a problem the Bach flower remedy Vervain should prove helpful. You will only need to use a very few drops and these can be added to your Taurus horse's drinking water. Kelp, (found in sea-weed supplements), is something you might also like to add to his feed. It is invaluable if he is run down and it will help to reduce the risk of a swollen thyroid gland. The tissue salt Nat Sulp. is often deficient in Taurus types. It is this which helps to eliminate fluids and prevent water retention. Chicory will help to reduce excess mucus and sage is soothing for throat irritation. These can all be added to the feed when necessary.

VIRGO

'She is so industrious, when she has nothing to do she sits and knits her brow!'
Anon.

Virgo, the second of the Earth signs is mutable earth. The action implied in the mutability of the sign enables it to adapt to changes. Although your Virgo horse or pony is unlikely to be able to 'knit her brows', or anything else for that matter, their Virgo nature creates in them the need to do something useful.

If your horse or pony was born in the Northern Hemisphere it is unlikely that Virgo will be his Sun sign. If it is, he must have been the result of a late foaling. It is more likely that if your horse has the Sun in Virgo, he was born in the early spring of the Southern Hemisphere. The Moon, however, is in the sign of Virgo for approximately two and a half days each month. His Moon in Virgo is therefore much more likely. Whichever is applicable the characteristics of Virgo will be apparent in his behaviour.

Naturally shy and retiring, your Virgo horse or pony will not push himself forward. Unless you encourage him to do otherwise he will be happy to stay in the background, carefully observing whatever is taking place around him.

Of all the signs of the zodiac, Virgo is the most diligent and hardworking. This is an animal who has abundant energy for hard work and who wants to serve you. Doing

angelica ~ caraway ~ dill ~ chamomile ~ fennel ~ cloves ~ chamomile ~ fennel ~ cloves ~ dill ~ caraway ~ angelica

so gives him a sense of well being and fulfilment. His vision is narrow and focussed. Once you have set him a task or goal he will do his very best to achieve it, paying attention to the most minute detail in order to get everything just right. You may be surprised by the very high standards he manages to achieve.

What the Virgo horse learns, he learns quickly and well. He will then be keen to put these skills to use in order to demonstrate his competence and capability. This makes him an ideal riding school horse or an excellent schoolmaster. However, a yard that lacks routine or feels chaotic will disturb him. No matter how well trained he may be, he will simply not be able to give of his best in such an environment. Instead, he will be fretful and inattentive. A busy and disorganised collecting ring could also make him nervous and jumpy. If this is so you would be wise to limit the time he has to spend there. Virgo horses feel most at ease when they are doing something productive, not when they are having to hang around doing nothing. Their nature is such that they need lots encouragement and praise if you are to get the best from them. Without such reassurance they will feel apprehensive and insecure.

Happy in any work that requires him to use his precision, dressage would suit your Virgo horse well. At work or at play he will persevere until he has everything just right. A Virgo horse with a Virgo rider could together spend so much time perfecting their skills they might never manage to get out of the practice ring.

Although the Virgo horse has the intelligence to cope with whatever you ask of him, he needs to know what he is doing. Not a risk taker, he is happiest with all that is tried and tested. Once he is properly trained he will have the confidence to show off his well developed skills. In their training as elsewhere in their lives, Virgo horses require order and routine. The repetitive training patterns necessary for eventing are something to which the Virgo temperament will respond well. But a horse born under this sign will need a very capable and disciplined rider to give him the courage he needs in order to cope with the unpredictable and the unknown features of an event course.

Relaxing is something your Virgo horse or pony will find difficult. His desire to be productive makes him a workaholic. It will be down to you to provide him with the type of gentle exercise and recreation that is a change and therefore a rest for him. As with the other earth signs, Taurus and Capricorn, the earth itself sustains and nourishes Virgo horse. Hacking him out in the countryside will do much to restore his vitality. Turning him out will have an instantly beneficial effect upon him. But remember his need to be productive: if boredom sets in because he is left for too long, he will set off in search of an occupation that might not be quite to your liking.

As mentioned earlier, the Virgo temperament is not well suited to 'muddle'. This horse needs order. His daily routine should be well ordered or he will become fretful. His living conditions should also be kept clean and tidy if he is to feel comfortable. The Virgo horse, more than any of the other signs will respond adversely to a stressful environment. Any situation in which he feels unsettled or under stress will have repercussions on his health. His unease will quickly become disease as he endeavours to communicate to you via his body, his unhappiness. Creating symptoms of the body are his way of gaining the care and attention he needs.

The areas of the Virgo horse's body most likely to be

problematic are the intestines and digestive tract. Weight loss and diarrhoea are sure signs of worry or fretfulness. Colic can be a more dangerous symptom of the same problem. All three can be avoided if he is given the correct care and lifestyle. When he feels well cared for, he can function efficiently. Virgo horses instinctively recognise their dependence upon the well being of the body. It needs to be well maintained if it is to operate efficiently. Therefore, they want to take good care of themselves, or will look to their owners to do it for them.

The astrological symbol for the sign of Virgo is the corn maiden, who is often depicted with a child on her knee and with wheat or bread in her hands. As such she is the image of fertility and productivity. A good mother, if perhaps rather fussy about her young, your Virgo mare will carefully encourage her foals to take care of themselves by teaching them to deal with the practical necessities of day to day living.

Diet is always important. For your Virgo horse or pony it is particularly so. He is likely to be a 'picky' eater carefully selecting what he knows is best for him. You could find that he even selects what he likes from his mix. Whoever said 'you are what you eat' was probably a Virgo. It certainly applies to your Virgo horse who could develop an allergic reaction to foods which do not suit him. High fibre foods are ideal. Recent research suggests that too much sugar can lead to an allergic reaction in some horses. Some feeds, such as oats and barley can cause allergic and other reactions. Your Virgo horse could become fizzy from eating oats and barley could cause lumps under the skin.

The Virgo horse or pony should respond well to natural and carefully measured homeopathic remedies. These can easily be added to the feed or administered straight from your hand, although they should be handled as little as possible. Nux. Vom. 6 is useful for nervous indigestion.

Virgo types should also respond well to herbs. The cleansing properties of dill, the ideal herb for Virgo, should prove beneficial. Angelica and caraway have a stimulating effect upon the digestive tract, should this be necessary. Fennel and cloves both clear the stomach of gasses and act as a disinfectant. Chamomile in either herb or pill form is a sedative and can be fed to horses or ponies prone to nervous colic.

The tissue salt for Virgo is Kali Sulph. (potassium sulphate). This can be helpful in preventing cracked hooves. It also assists in keeping the coat and skin healthy. Carrots are a natural source of this tissue salt.

CAPRICORN

'slowly and surely, slowly and surely, he made his way down to the river'
Aesop's Fables. The Hare and The Tortoise.

*"'Have you all got something?' asked Christopher Robin.
'All except me' said Eeyore. 'As Usual'".
He looked round at them in his melancholy way.*
Winnie-the-Pooh. A. A. Milne.

comfrey ~ calcium phosphate ~ calendula ~ frankincense ~ hemp ~ cloves ~ calcium phosphate ~ cloves ~ comfrey ~ frankincense ~ calendula

If your horse, or pony, was born when the Sun or the Moon was in the sign of Capricorn you perhaps recognise in him the melancholic temperament which epitomises Eeyore. The pessimistic and gloomy attitude which is so much a part of his character will perhaps be apparent in him from time to time, especially if he is not given the reassurance he so badly needs. Although his bearing is very dignified, more than any of the other signs of the zodiac, your Capricorn is filled with doubt and uncertainty. This can act as a spur to great achievement or can inhibit progress. Your Capricorn companion wants very much to do well. In this way he shows you that he is worthy of your care. But his fearful and doubtful nature needs plenty of encouragement and praise if he is to achieve his potential. Given this, he will work diligently to reward your efforts. Without it Capricorn horse will be unable to meet the challenges you set him. Instead he will become the dull and forlorn Eeyore going round and round in circles, but getting nowhere.

Capricorn is the third and last earth sign and is ruled by the planet Saturn. In mythology Saturn (also known as Kronos) is the god connected with time, timing, limits, boundaries and structure. He bestowed an understanding of necessity, duty and obligation. Embodying such qualities, this cardinal earth sign initiates carefully structured and well-timed action.

A Capricorn horse or pony cannot be hurried. What he learns, he learns thoroughly, but does so in his own time. He instinctively knows the dangers that accompany the tendency to rush things, or to cut corners. In this, he resembles the tortoise not the hare. Capricorn horse prefers to take things one step at a time, building slowly but surely on each subsequent success. If you rush him, you will not get the best from him.

Caution, an inherent trait in the sign of Capricorn, will colour your Capricorn horse's behaviour and his response. The unpredictability of a day out hunting will for him be fraught with obstacles and dangers. His cautious approach could be your saving. With a plucky rider who is brave enough to ride over fences with confidence, Capricorn horse may well get home without any accidents. But he could just as easily hesitate at the first fence, and flatly refuse to take his rider any further. By the same token, however, once he knows an event course – with a confident rider he should do well; but don't present him with too many surprises if you want to remain seated.

This is an animal who is capable of tremendous hard work and persistent effort. In his early training, it is important to treat him with discipline and sensitivity. Capricorn horses will thrive on structure and routine but will shy away from harsh criticism. A carefully planned training programme designed with consideration for his well being will reap its rewards. But if your ambition for his success is too great, or you are too impatient, pushing him on before he is ready, you will inhibit his progress. The outcome will be a fretful and highly-strung mess.

Your Capricorn horse or pony is not a risk taker. He gains his confidence from what has been tried and tested. It is therefore better if he is handled and ridden by the same person each day, rather than having a variety of different owners or grooms. Anything new or innovative will arouse his suspicion and make him feel wary. Once something becomes familiar to him, he will feel at ease with it. An environment which is foreign to him will be unsettling. Capricorn horse is neither a natural hunter nor eventer. If put in any situation where he is asked to take a risk, or to confront the unpredictable – he could just freeze to the spot.

From all this, it perhaps seems strange that most racehorses are born while the Sun is in the sign of Capricorn. A horse who 'freezes' at the first fence is after all, unlikely to romp home with the glittering prizes. However, the qualifier who will not jump a stick out hunting will often be a demon on the racecourse, where he knows 'what the form is'!

Thoroughbreds, who are aged from the 1st January each year, were originally bred for speed and for racing. The closer they are born to this date the better it is for their owners. The ideal Thoroughbred should be fast and active, bold, brave and spirited. But as you can see from what you have read so far, Capricorn doesn't really bestow the ideal temperament for racing. However, the Capricorn's ability to put effort and determination into whatever he does will help him to stay the course. He will need to know the job well if he is to feel at ease with it. Familiarity and appropriate training will stand him in good stead. But without a favourable moon sign, or other astrological indicators of fast and competitive characteristics, no matter how willing he may be, he is unlikely to be a winner.

It is of help when the Capricorn racehorse is born with the Moon in one of the fire signs, ideally Aries or Sagittarius, or in the swift and agile air sign Gemini.

Arabs, from whom all Thoroughbreds descend, are also bred for racing. But they are much tougher animals.

Designed to cross vast planes of sand they have the ability to endure over long distances. Their endurance and stamina is much more in keeping with the qualities of the earth signs. However, the Arab is also blessed with the fast and free-floating action and the bold spirited intelligence more commonly associated with the elements of air and fire. It might be useful to take these things into consideration if you are looking at the breeding lines of a horse for racing.

Jockies who are overly competitive and courageous and who perhaps have Aries or Gemini characteristics are more likely to get the best from any racehorse born under Capricorn.

The sign of Capricorn rules the skin, the skeleton and the teeth. All three are potentially problem areas for your Capricorn horse or pony. Ensure that his teeth are checked regularly. Dental problems could affect his ability to take in the nourishment he requires to stay well. If he is over-worked or pushed too hard your Capricorn horse might well develop a rigid and inflexible attitude towards his work. This will be reflected in general stiffness and in joint problems, particularly in the hocks. As movement helps to maintain flexibility, keeping a Capricorn horse in a confined space for any length of time could be detrimental to him. Exercise that is relaxing and fun will be beneficial, as long as the fun doesn't border on frivolity!

Your Capricorn will probably not eat when he is stressed. If he does, it could result in colicky symptoms. The tissue salt suitable for Capricorn types is Calcium Phosphate, which builds and strengthens teeth and bones.

A deficiency of this salt will lead to poor digestion and will inhibit the distribution of albumen. This in turn can lead to kidney stones, dental problems, and possible crystallisation of joints. Calcium and phosphorous are the two major minerals fed to horses. They are essential to their well being and are therefore included in all compound feeds. They are also added to mineral licks and to supplements such as dicalcium phosphate and limestone flour. Calcium phosphate is naturally found in wheat, barley and rye, peas, beans and milk products. Tension can reduce its absorption.

Any inability to fully eliminate toxins can lead to skin problems which can also be a sign of stress, tension and disease, particularly if your horse is subjected to an environment which is not conducive to his needs.

Frankincense tincture administered externally is antiseptic, cleansing and astringent agent. Its anti-inflammatory properties are valuable in assisting the rapid healing of cuts, wounds and abrasions. Oil of cloves is a known remedy for tooth pain.

As a foal your Capricorn will seem to have an old head on a young body. His calm and sensible character will make him easy to handle and to train. This makes him an ideal children's horse or pony. Wise beyond his years, he should, with the passing of time grow into his age, enjoying his productive years and settling later on into a contented retirement.

CHAPTER 4

THE AIR SIGNS

THE THREE AIR SIGNS are Gemini, Libra and Aquarius. All three are concerned with rational thought and communication.

Air is social and ethereal. It cannot be tied down.

The element of air is associated with the life force – the breath. It is linked to ideas, and is experienced as intelligence. The air signs are able to detach themselves in order to gain perspective. This allows for objectivity but can appear to be uncaring and aloof.

Air signs do not cope well with restriction. They are inclined to be fickle. They like to know that they can move easily from one thing to another when the mood takes them

★ Gemini is the mutable air sign. It flits from one thing to another with speed and alacrity.

★ Libra is the cardinal air sign. It will initiate relation ships in order to share experience.

★ Aquarius is the fixed air sign. It is inventive and experimental. It is also rather stubborn.

If your horse or pony was born when either the Sun or the Moon was in an air sign, he will be an intelligent, freedom-loving creature who will need the company of others.

GEMINI

*'Rabbit had to go away,' said Pooh. 'I think he thought of
something he had to go and see about suddenly.'*
  Winnie-the-Pooh. A. A. Milne

sunflower~kelp~garlic~

lavender~chamomile~horseradish

horseradish~chamomile~lavender

garlic~kelp~sunflower~

Gemini is the first of the three air signs and it is mutable which means that it adapts very easily to change.

If your horse or pony was born when either the Sun or the Moon was in the sign of Gemini it is quite likely that you recognise in him a propensity to suddenly move from one thing to another or from one place to another, just because something more interesting attracts his attention.

When the characteristics of Gemini are emphasised in your horse's temperament, he easily becomes distracted. Inclined to flit from one thing to another, (unless his interest is engaged), he will become very restless. Boredom is his worse enemy. When he has nothing to occupy his mind, or to satisfy his curiosity, he will look for something. And you can bet that nine times out of ten the 'something' will be mischief. For the Gemini horse, the grass really is greener on the other side of the fence – and he is more than able to use his natural agility in order to get to it. Once a notion is in his head very little will stop him. It will be easier for you if you can pre-empt this by keeping him occupied.

The key to a Gemini horse's well being is variety. More than any other sign of the zodiac, your Gemini needs the stimulus of a busy and varied environment if he is to thrive. A yard where there is plenty going on is ideal. Far from fretting if he has to move to a different stable, or graze a different field, he will enjoy being somewhere new and different. He will also relish the company of new friends, especially if he is able to learn a new trick or two from them!

In your Gemini horse or pony, you have a companion

who will really love to be taken out. The more 'too-ing' and 'fro-ing' you do with him, the better he will like it. Just the sound of your horsebox engine will be enough to have him on his toes. Given a trailer or lorry which is light and airy with sight of a way out, loading him should be a 'breeze'. Leaving him behind in favour of a stable mate could prove more difficult. Unless you can provide him with a suitable distraction you just could come home to a ruined stable door or an empty paddock.

This highly intelligent creature learns easily. He is interested in everything. His mind and his body are quick and agile; his movements light and swift. Rather like the god Mercury, who rules the sign of Gemini, he appears to have wings on his feet. This makes him perfectly suited to any work which requires him jump at speed. However, the Gemini horse's highly-strung nervous system is prone to tension and stress. Ever alert, he is easily spooked. His gift of flight can then turn to flightiness, and his jumping skills to jumpiness. The best way to avoid agitation, irritability and neurosis is to channel his abundant nervous energy into work which occupies him both physically and mentally

The speed and agility of your Gemini pony should put him in the lead on the polo field or in any other discipline that requires swift and nimble movement, such as Point to Pointing or Scurry Driving. His eye and limb co-ordination should be good. However, unless other astrological factors suggest the contrary, his inability to remain focussed for any length of time is his weakness. As an Eventer he should do well at jumping and cross-country but is likely to fall down on the dressage test because he lacks the necessary concentration and precision. A rider who knows the test well and has the skills to keep him on track will do much to mitigate this flaw, but even then a distraction outside the arena could be enough to loose precious marks and ruin it for both of you.

From what you have read so far, you can perhaps see that the Gemini horse or pony is not an animal who will do well in an environment where he has to be boxed in or has to live on his own. He is extremely sociable and needs plenty of space. Without room to move and fresh air to breathe he will become miserable and unhappy. This could then lead to rapid weight loss. If he has to be tied up or shut in for any length of time the Gemini horse can become restless and highly-strung, inclined as he is to literally 'run a mile' from routine and drudgery. Under these circumstances, he will then resort to very destructive behaviour.

The sign of Gemini rules the limbs, the lungs and the nervous system. The nervous system communicates messages from the brain to the rest of the body. When it malfunctions, the body registers the problem via body ailments.

Whilst your Gemini horse or pony needs to be mentally and physically occupied, his abundant nervous energy makes it difficult for him to wind down. Overactivity can then result in nervous exhaustion. It will help him if you can balance his exercise so that some of what he does is both stimulating and relaxing. If you are lucky enough to have access to plenty of rides or bridle paths, hacking him out somewhere different each day will do much to achieve this. Muscular aches and pains can be relieved by massage. Aromatherapy massage with lavender oil is particularly valuable for the Gemini temperament. Chiropractics or osteopathy can prove beneficial for more serious back and shoulder problems. Because a Gemini horse's lungs are sensitive, dust in his hay or in his environment can be more than usually problematic. It is therefore essential that you avoid mouldy hay and soak any that is likely to be dusty.

Potassium Chloride (Kali.Mur.) is the tissue salt which is often deficient in Gemini types. It is a blood conditioner and it also helps to prevent lung troubles. A deficiency can lead to difficulty in shaking off coughs and colds which can, in extreme circumstances develop into pleurisy or pneumonia. Maize is a natural source of this salt.

Due to his highly strung temperament, the Gemini horse and pony is prone to sweating, especially when he is nervous. Any horse who sweats a lot needs extra potassium chloride if he is to avoid diaphragmatic thumps. Commercially known as low salt, this tissue salt is available as a feed supplement. It can also be administered in tablet form. Kelp and seaweed are excellent natural sources of potassium chloride. In their dried form they can be added to the feed. They also provide dietary calcium valuable to young horses and to those who are old and fatigued.

Garlic is a wonderful natural remedy for chest and lung problems. Mixing your horse's feed with water which has been infused with a few cloves of garlic is an easy way of administering it daily. Otherwise it can be added to the feed crushed, or in its powdered or tablet form. Horseradish root also contains properties which assist in the curing of coughs and colds.

Sunflower oil, which can be added to the feed, is a helpful remedy for all bronchial troubles. Nettle purifies the blood and is readily available in pastures that have not been treated with weed killers. Lavender, the herb of Gemini, is a relaxant and nerve soother. Also known for its antiseptic properties, as well as being used in its oil form for massage, it can easily be grown in pots and hanging baskets around the yard where its scent can permeate the air. Chamomile is said to have sedative properties beneficial to the nervous or highly- strung horse or pony and is often fed to those prone to nervous colic. It can be administered in homeopathic pill form or added as a herb to his feed.

Given the right environment and care, your Gemini horse or pony will stay young and athletic well into old age, giving you joy and companionship for many years to come.

LIBRA

'It isn't much fun for One, but Two
Can stick together,' says Pooh, says he.
'That's how it is,' says Pooh.
Winnie-the-Pooh. A. A. Milne.

Libra, the second of the three Air signs, is ruled by the planet Venus and is symbolised by the scales. The balance, beauty, harmony and love so essential to this sign are satisfied by being in a close relationship with another. By being in a partnership the Libra spirit can enjoy shared experi-

parsley ~ sodium ~ thyme

dandelion ~ horseradish ~ chamomile ~

chamomile ~ dandelion ~ horseradish

thyme ~ sodium ~ parsley ~

ence. A cardinal sign, it also needs to work towards something. It is goal oriented.

The sign of Libra covers the time of the year when, in the Northern Hemisphere, the nights are getting longer and it is time to wind down. The shorter days and the colder weather are not ideal for foaling and for rearing young foals. It is therefore unusual for horses or ponies to be born when the Sun is in the sign of Libra. However, as the Moon is in Libra for approximately two and a half days every month, a Libra Moon is a much more likely prospect. Or perhaps you are the owner of a horse or pony born in the Southern Hemisphere where Libra heralds the spring.

If either the Sun or the Moon were in the sign of Libra when your horse or pony was born, he will display Libra behaviour and characteristics, the most obvious of which will be his great reluctance to be alone. Isolation is his real dread. Without a friend or companion his life is unbalanced. Such an imbalance will have a direct affect upon his behaviour and his health. A lonely Libra is a very sorry character. He is therefore best suited to a lifestyle where he can enjoy your company and ideally the companionship of another horse, pony or donkey. A friend really will make all the difference in the world to his ability to thrive.

Disharmony will distress the Libra horse. He wants to please you and to know that you are pleased with him. If he is subjected to harsh or aggressive treatment he really will suffer, becoming very morose and brooding. The emotional imbalance will then make itself felt physically through kidney and urinary tract problems, or in extreme, cases diabetes.

As an air sign your Libra horse or pony needs to be out in the open. He will not enjoy being shut in for long periods of time and he needs plenty of regular exercise. In situations where he can join you in a shared experience he will be at his best. He is the perfect partner for anyone who understands his sensitive nature and who treats him with the kindness and the consideration he deserves. Ask him nicely and he will soon be eating out of your hand, metaphorically as well as literally. A natural 'gentleman', this horse can charm the birds out of the trees. His innate good manners will enable you to take him anywhere. Everyone will love him.

The down side to this intelligent and considerate animal is laziness. His easy-going temperament needs plenty of gentle encouragement. He is extremely capable but does not believe in overexerting himself – unless there is something in it for him. That 'something' can be as little as your pleasure and recognition of his efforts. With this particular companion, a hug will bring big results, as will the occasional tasty morsel. He needs to know you care.

The Libra horse's sensitivity to his environment is pronounced. He needs beauty; it restores his soul. The natural beauty of the countryside will do much to maintain his well being. A dirty, shabby or untidy home will have quite the reverse effect. More than any of the other signs of the zodiac, your Libra horse or pony should not be expected to live or work in conditions which are not congenial to him. Nor should he be with people who are not in harmony with him and his needs.

Not really suited to anything that is risky or highly competitive, the Libra horse is better suited to work which involves him and you in a one-to-one partnership of strategy. He should do well as a dressage horse, rising to the opportunity to display his skills with grace and intelligence. He should also enjoy driving, especially in co-operation with another horse or pony. His temperament is made for being one of a pair. But don't subject him to anything which requires him to be quick and decisive. Put on the spot, he will dither. Given a choice between two routes he will want to take them both.

A balanced diet is important to the well being of the Libra horse, especially the balance between acids and alkalis. Sodium Phosphate, the Libra tissue salt, can do much to maintain this balance as it neutralises acid. Sodium and phosphorous are two of the four main minerals essential to horses and ponies. Along with the other two, calcium and magnesium they are present in mineral licks and are added to compound feeds. Sodium Phosphate is also naturally present in carrots, apples and wheat.

With the right care and living conditions, your Libra horse or pony should enjoy robust good health. However, the kidneys and the lumbar region of the spine are the two main areas of the body where your Libra horse is vulnerable, and it is here via physical symptoms that any imbalance or disease might register. Massage, especially aromatherapy massage can help to relieve tension in the lumbar region and can be very relaxing. Because the kidneys are vulnerable the Libra horse should always have access to plenty of fresh water. Should he develop a urinary tract infection it could upset the electrolyte balance in his body, making the excretion of waste products more difficult. A variety of symptoms involving the digestive tract, heart and nervous system can then arise. Damage to the kidneys can lead to renal failure which is extremely severe and can be life threatening.

Sodium Phosphate will revitalise the kidneys. Parsley and dandelion both contain properties which can help prevent kidney disorders. So can horseradish root, a diuretic which promotes perspiration, thus assisting with the elimination of toxins. Chamomile is the homeopathic remedy most suited to the restless and indecisive qualities of the Libra temperament. It is also available in herb form and is said to have sedative properties. But the herb most beneficial of all to Libra is Thyme. A note of warning however, Thyme should not be picked from near roads as it easily absorbs lead.

AQUARIUS

'Twas brillig and the slithy toves
Did gyre and gimble in the wabe;
All mimsy were the borogroves
And the mome raths outgrabe.'
The Jabberwocky. Lewis Carroll.

Trying to make sense of your Aquarius horse or pony will be as difficult as trying to make sense out of the rhyme above. Just when you think you have him 'sussed', he will do something totally out of the blue which will leave you completely bewildered. As the owner of this bright and intelligent animal you will need to learn – to expect the unexpected.

Ruled by the planets Saturn and Uranus your Aquarius

caraway ~ rosemary ~ mayweed ~ silica ~ bryonia ~ rosemary ~ caraway ~ nettle ~ hyssop ~ silica ~ bryonia

horse or pony is an enigma. He is both stubborn and inconsistent, reliable and unpredictable, loyal and freedom loving, independent yet one of the team. Neither he nor his erratic behaviour is at all easy to understand.

Aquarius is the last of the three air signs. In keeping

with the other air signs, Gemini and Libra, he needs to share his experiences. But because Aquarius is a fixed sign, he is inclined to be rather rigid in his attitude. At the same time the Aquarius horse is fuelled by high voltage electrical energy which makes him nervous and highly strung. Rather like an electric circuit, his nervous system is inclined to cut out or blow a fuse if it is overloaded. However, it is possible to syphon off some of his nervous energy by channelling it into his work – so long as the work is neither boring nor too repetitive. Here is an animal who needs the excitement and stimulus of something new if he is to remain interested and focussed. Experiment with his training programme. Introduce new techniques and he will rise to the challenge. But follow the same methods day after day, and you will be asking for trouble.

All three of the air signs enjoy the breath and freedom of the great outdoors. Once he is outside your Aquarius companion will find plenty to satisfy his curiosity. A mental gymnast, there is no end to his fascination in every new thing he comes across. Physically he is less keen. There will be days when it takes a complete crisis to spur him into action.

Essentially, your Aquarius horse or pony dislikes being told what to do. While he will benefit from disciplined handling, he actually prefers to do things his own way. This is part of the dichotomy of owning such an eccentric creature. He is an individual. As such he should be given the means to express his individuality. His stubborn and rebellious spirit instinctively resists orders and commands, even when they are issued nicely. You can use your best endeavours to persuade him to do things your way. But the minute you are distracted or your back is turned, he will adapt whatever you told him – to his way of doing things.

Training such a strong willed and unpredictable creature requires great skill. Unless his interest is engaged he is easily distracted. You can never be sure what he will do next. Force will not work. It will only produce even greater resistance. Within the limits and the structure of his environment and his routine the Aquarius horse needs to feel free. Mentally agile, his mind moves with lightening speed from one thing to another. You will need to use your wits to keep him focussed. Apparently unable to understand what it is you are asking of him, suddenly he will get the message and then there will be no stopping him. When he understands, he understands completely. Once he has grasped what you want from him he has the intelligence and the determination to perform the task with dedication and brilliance.

For his happiness and your comfort, handle this animal firmly but kindly. Ensure that his training programme is varied and interesting, then turn him out to do his own thing.

It is perhaps apparent that this strong and unpredictable animal is not a novice ride. Although he is loving and can be very amusing he needs an experienced owner to cope with his rebellious streak and his strong need for freedom.

The sociable nature of an Aquarius horse means that he is most at home in an environment where he can enjoy the company of human and equine friends. He needs to know that he is one of the gang — as long as this is not at the expense of his much needed individuality. When you ask him to conform, to work in line with the rest of the team, it might take a while for you to realise that he is the only one in step. Ideally he should be somewhere like a busy racing yard, where he is in the company of other horses but where his performance depends upon his own merits.

The Moon is in the sign of Aquarius for approximately two and a half days each month. The Sun is in the sign of Aquarius from approximately January 21st until February 18th each year. If your horse or pony was born in the northern hemisphere when the sun was in the sign of Aquarius he will have been born within the peak breeding time for thoroughbreds, most of whom are destined to become racehorses. Blessed with a strong body which is both swift and agile, if the Aquarius horse is trained well and then given his head, it is within his scope to break new ground and new records.

Similarly if his eccentricity is accepted and he is allowed to perform, with a skilled rider he should make an excellent show jumper. In freestyle showing he will also come into his own as long as he is accustomed to having his routine changed regularly. His endurance and his love of change will enable him to get the best out of any discipline that requires such attributes.

Although he appears calm and docile on the surface, this highly charged animal is a bundle of nervous energy underneath. His unpredictable response can produce sudden bursts of strenuous activity. It can also make him accident prone. His lower limbs, in particular his cannon bones and fetlocks, are vulnerable to injury. Sprains and strains to his fetlocks and pasterns are likely to occur with frustrating regularity if he is overworked. His fetlocks are also susceptible to swellings and to the accumulation of fluid in their joints. Caraway can help to strengthen sprained limbs. The homeopathic remedy Rhus Tox in its tincture form is an invaluable first aid treatment for sprains and strains.

The Aquarius temperament is prone to high blood pressure, circulation problems and muscle cramps. Plenty of fresh air and strenuous exercise is extremely beneficial as both will naturally oxygenate the blood and improve the circulation. Massage will help to relieve muscular aches and pains and will act as a relaxant when your horse or pony is wound up. Poor circulation can lead to laminitis, navicular and bone changes in the hoof. The homeopathic remedy Bryonia can be very helpful if it is administered early on, when the inflammation is acute. Silicea is recommended when the condition is more established. In either case it would be advisable to first consult a vet who is trained in homeopathy.

Rosemary is the herb most suited to the Aquarius temperament. Added to the diet it stimulates the circulation and helps to reduce high blood pressure. Hyssop, often found growing in the wild also helps to regulate blood pressure. Added to the feed it can help to reduce anxiety and nervous tension. In its oil form it can be used to reduce bruising. Nettle, naturally available in pasture that has not been treated with weed killers, improves circulation and helps to purify the blood.

The tissue salt for Aquarius is Sodium chloride (Nat Mur.). Sodium chloride (natural salt) balances the body's water content. Your Aquarius horse or pony is likely to be deficient in this salt because it is so easily eliminated from his body. A deficiency causes watery eyes and nostrils, dry skin and dry mucous membranes. It also slows down the digestive system. Although it is available in pill form, natural sources of this tissue salt are carrots and apples which can easily be chopped up and given as part of the feed.

CHAPTER 5

THE WATER SIGNS

THE THREE WATER SIGNS, Cancer, Scorpio and Pisces are all connected with the feelings. Because of this, all three water signs are particularly in tune with nuances and subtleties. Their enhanced intuition governs their behaviour and their response. It makes them unusually receptive to the threat of danger. It also enables them to pick up on the moods and feelings of those around them. Like water itself, those born under the signs of Cancer, Scorpio and Pisces, lack a shape and solidity of their own, and their natural fluidity needs to be contained. This is best done by someone who is practical and down to earth – someone who can guide and channel their energy into something solid and concrete. For this reason they are happiest in the care of an owner whose capability, reliability and dependability gives them a feeling of safety. They are not comfortable around people who are too exuberant, or too detached. The sensitivity of the water signs is so pronounced that they will wilt under harsh or judgmental treatment. All three instinctively protect them-selves from anything that threatens their survival.

Their means of self-protection is individual to their particular sign.

* Cancer, the first of the water signs, is cardinal. It is the water sign that most readily acts on its feelings.
* Scorpio, the second of the water signs, is fixed. The fixity adds depth and determination to its already sensitive nature.
* Pisces, the last of the water signs, is mutable. It is the most adaptable and impressionable of the three.

If your horse or pony was born when either the Sun or the Moon was in one of the water signs, he or she will be a gentle and sensitive companion who requires quiet handling and plenty of human contact.

CANCER

'The smell of that buttered toast simply talked to Toad, and with no uncertain voice; talked of warm kitchens, of breakfasts on bright frosty mornings, of cosy parlour firesides on winter evenings'.
The Wind In The Willows. Kenneth Grahame.

If you are the owner of a Cancer horse or pony he might not salivate at the smell of buttered toast or know what a cosy parlour fireside is, but he will most certainly enjoy his food and the comfort of his own stable. Cancer is the sign of the zodiac that more than any other is associated with hearth and home, caring, feeding and nurturing.

Ruled by the Moon, you might find that the behaviour of your Cancer horse or pony does actually change with

raspberry ~ hops ~ arnica

dandelion ~ chicory ~ horseradish

arnica ~ hops ~ raspberry

dandelion ~ chicory ~ horseradish

the phases of the Moon, the changes being particularly evident on a New or a Full Moon. Whether or not this is the case, he is a creature whose moods and responses will wax and wane. How he feels will have a direct affect upon his behaviour and his work will reflect this inherent inconsistency. One day your Cancer horse will be keen, alert, attentive and responsive, giving you all you ask of him. The next day, you may be struggling to get him out of the yard such will be the lack of enthusiasm. On days like these battling with a Cancer horse is a waste of your time and energy. He is a non-confrontational animal and dislikes a fight. Insist on obedience and he will yield to your demands (albeit unwillingly) . However, having won the battle, you could find his lack of involvement in what he is doing (matched by an equal lack of responsiveness to your commands), leaves you feeling frustrated and worn out. As you decide to give up and call it a day, you might feel that although having won the battle you have lost the war. Perhaps your time would have been better spent on a gentle hack around the fields.

The indirect and non-confrontational aspect of the Cancer temperament means that this horse quite literally takes a sideways approach to things. Watch him in the field. He will automatically circumvent obstacles. In the arena or show ring under clear direction he can move forward in straight lines, but loose contact with him and he will zig-zag all over the place, emulating your uncertainty or lack of concentration.

Because his nature is so fluid, your Cancer horse or pony lacks a direction and a focus of his own. He has abundant energy and tremendous sensitivity but requires practised handling and is not a novice ride. Cancer horse's acute receptivity will immediately pick up on fear or apprehension, no matter how slight. Lack of guidance and control will leave him feeling nervous and insecure. Instead he needs a rider who can instil in him the focus and direction which he lacks; someone whose competence and confidence can harness and channel his sensitivity and exuberance.

The fluidity of a Cancer horse's nature can easily be moulded into whatever you want him to be. If you acquire him when he is a foal he will be receptive to your every wish. But because he is ultra sensitive he can just as easily be ruined by poor handling. Cancer youngstock who are treated harshly or cruelly will remember and respond accordingly in the future. They will become snappy or will withdraw into themselves. Similarly, Cancer youngsters can quickly pick up bad habits which are difficult to correct once they are established.

The vulnerability of Cancer horses is not weakness, but is evidence of their tremendous sensitivity. Careful handling by an equally sensitive and receptive owner will bring out the best in them, producing remarkable results.

Whilst Cancer horse can exist quite happily without the company of other horses, more than anything else he needs human contact. Your Cancer companion will become very fretful if he has to spend long periods of time without you. You are his surrogate mother and as such, you represent survival. His bond with you is a very close one. Where you go he will follow (whenever this is possible). Without your care and attention he will become sad and withdrawn. By handling and grooming him regularly you can give him the reassurance he requires.

Next to your warm care and attention, food is probably the second most important thing in a Cancer horse's life. Not only does it give him essential nourishment, but it tells him that he is loved. Because of this, he should be fed at the same time each day and in the same place. The routine helps make him feel secure. Cancer horse is extremely possessive of anything that means security to him. Forget to feed him on time and he is likely to go into the most incredible sulk, turning his back on you and shutting you out. Allow another horse or pony to get to his feed bucket before he does and you will be amazed by the ferocity of his response. A love of food makes Cancer horses greedy. If you are able to control what they eat all should be well. But given *ad lib* grazing on rich pasture they can easily put on weight. In spring and summer your greedy Cancer pony needs particularly careful management because he is an ideal candidate for laminitis.

A natural mother who will care for and nurture her offspring, in your Cancer horse or pony you have the perfect brood mare. Her 'nest making' instinct is strong. When she has someone or something to look after in the safety of her own 'home' she is at her best. But don't forget her possessive streak. Without careful weaning she will become very distressed when her foals are taken from her. The homeopathic remedy Arnica is useful during and after pregnancy. Raspberry is a feed additive commonly used on studs because it is known to aid parturition in mares. The leaves are often fed for two months prior to foaling to improve muscle tone and stimulate good milk yield.

The sign of Cancer rules the breasts, it would therefore

be wise to be alert to early symptoms of mastitis in your brood mare.

The sensitive nature of your Cancer horse or pony and his protective instinct means that once trained he will take excellent care of his rider. Given confident handling he will do well working with disabled riders. In his maturity, with adequate training he will also make an excellent schoolmaster. Cancer horses instinctively respond to the subtle commands of dressage, and their ability to listen and respond quickly makes them good at showjumping, in skilled hands.

Your Cancer horse or pony is suspicious of anything new so being away from home can be a very stressful experience for him. By travelling him in the same vehicle each time and by bringing him home to the same place, you can do much to alleviate this anxiety.

Cancer horses do well in a calm environment where they can enjoy the familiarity of their own rider own stable and ideally own yard. For them this is far better than a busy yard. The hustle and bustle of a environment where there is lots of noise and a lack of structure will make a Cancer horse feel nervous and uncertain. His distress will make itself known via behavioural problems and digestive disorders. He is a natural worrier who should not be fed when he is anxious or stressed. By staying and waiting until he has calmed down, you may help avoid digestive problems such as gastritis, constipation or colic.

Dandelion, readily available in pasture which has not been treated with weed killers, has a slight laxative effect and is helpful in eliminating toxins from the body. Chicory and fenugreek are natural remedies known to help soothe and calm stomach inflammation. These can be bought as herbal supplements. Probiotics, available in paste or powder form, is an excellent cure for diarrhoea caused by stress.

The homeopathic remedy Nux. Vom. 6c is a useful remedy for stomach upsets. Colchicum 6c is useful for flatulent colic and is recommended by some vets for treating cases of spasmodic colic.

Dried hops make an excellent tonic for the horse or pony who worries a lot, or gets fractious when he is away from home. Because of its sedative effect it should not be administered without the advice of a specialist. Nor should it be given to breeding stock, due to the affect it has on the hormonal system.

Regular exercise is obviously beneficial because it helps to keep your Cancer horse or pony supple and fights the tendency to put on weight. Massage can help to eliminate fluid, which Cancer horses are inclined to retain. Horseradish root is an excellent diuretic. Clac Fluor. (Fluoride of Lime) is the tissue salt often deficient in Cancer types. Lack of it can lead to loss of muscle tone. It is available in pill form and can be administered from the hand or added to the feed.

SCORPIO

*"The question is '..which is to be the master'
that's all."*
    Lewis Carroll.

chicory ~ arnica ~ kelp ~
~garlic ~ seaweed ~ sulphate of lime
~kelp ~ arnica ~ chicory ~ garlic ~ seaweed ~ sulphate of lime

Unless your horse or pony was born in the southern hemisphere it is unlikely that he will have been born when the Sun was in the sign of Scorpio. By November the days in the northern hemisphere are too short and too cold for foaling. However, the Moon is in the sign of Scorpio for approximately two and a half days every month. It is therefore possible that he has a Scorpio Moon.

If you are the owner of a Scorpio horse or pony you will identify only too well with this quote from 'Alice'. Which one of you is to be the master will dominate your relationship. Scorpio, the second of the water signs, is fixed water. Ruled by the planets Mars and Pluto it bestows upon your worthy steed an extremely strong personality. Courageous, determined, purposeful and persevering, he is indeed masterful. While this is a distinct advantage when it is applied to his work, when these same characteristics are pitted *against* you, you need to be a match for him.

Although on the surface Scorpio horse might appear quiet, beneath this calm exterior rages a veritable torrent of explosive energy. Because he is fuelled by this reservoir of high emotional intensity, he puts his heart into everything he does. For your Scorpio horse, it is all or nothing. When such forceful energy is channelled into his work there is no stopping him. The strong and compact build of these horses is suggestive of the concentrated power and strength that enables them to keep going for as long as you need them to. But if this same forceful determination is not channelled it can be very destructive. Scorpio horse is not a good choice for a weak or indecisive owner. His acute intuition will immediately pick up on your uncertainty and you will be beaten before you start Vascilate and you will discover just how adept he is at using a strong will to control you. With this particular horse or pony you have your work cut out. He is indeed a challenge.

If this sounds like the 'horse from hell' take heart. Unless you have only just acquired him you will know by now that your Scorpio horse also has a good side and that his fighting spirit is only used when he is feeling vulnerable or afraid. It all stems from the 'beat them before they beat me' sentiment which can be avoided if you handle your horse properly. True, he enjoys a fight and is not a good looser; but his enormous courage is matched by his honesty which makes him very genuine. Granted, he is bigger and stronger than you are but he respects firmness. Handle him with kindness and don't let his behaviour dictate to you. Remember you are the boss. Make the rules and then stick to them. If your Scorpio horse senses a weakening of your resolve, he will trample all over you. At worse this could be literally so. You have to use your brain not your brawn. With a confident and competent handler he will learn quickly and go from strength to strength.

Wise beyond his years, your Scorpio horse or pony is deeply instinctual and uncannily perceptive. He instantly senses who is and is not to be trusted and will react accordingly. Whilst his naturally suspicious nature is slow to warm to people, once he trusts you he will be totally loyal to you. Betray that trust and he will never forget it. Be forewarned, the perception of ensuing insecurity will then bring out the very worst in him.

The 'feeling' nature of all the water signs signify that

your Scorpio horse or pony will need lots of love and care. Once he feels secure, he will develop a deep bond with you which will be extremely rewarding. He senses how you are feeling and will at times absorb those feelings, becoming despondent when you feel low and enthusiastic when you are happy.

Because a Scorpio horse finds it hard to resist temptation, you would do well to keep it out of his way. Ensure that his living environment is a secure one. Small and intimate will suit him better than large and bustling. Familiarity is also important to his sense of safety. Scorpio horses does not like having changes imposed upon them and will literally dig their heels in whenever you try to move them to somewhere new.

The intensity of Scorpio horse's nature needs to be balanced with plenty of rest and relaxation. By all means work him hard but then give him time to play. Although he will be happy being stabled, he will find being turned out very restorative because it puts him back in touch with nature. Massage can be an extremely effective treatment for overworked or strained muscles, whilst Arnica 6c is the homeopathic remedy which is most suitable for stiffness and muscle strain in the Scorpio horse.

Any activity which requires staying power suits the Scorpio horse. Endurance and long distance riding are two disciplines in which he will shine. His tremendous strength and determination make him more than able to cope the rigours of this sort of work and he will easily outlast the competition. This enormous facility for endurance coupled with a passion and bravery makes your Scorpio horse the perfect mount for riding across country.

The sign of Scorpio rules the bladder, rectum, pelvis, sexual organs and generative system. All are vulnerable when this particular type of horse or pony is under stress. Constipation and impaction is something from which he is likely to suffer but their likelihood can be reduced by giving him plenty of exercise and making sure he always has access to plenty of fresh water. Chicory, which can be added to the feed, is an effective, gentle laxative. It aids recovery from overwork and strain, so is always valuable to the Scorpio makeup. Kelp or seaweed is also a mild laxative. Available in powder form, it can help reduce flatulent colic, promotes a healthy coat and strengthens hooves. Hernias are something else to watch out for in Scorpio horses and ponies who may be more than usually susceptible to them. They are also prone to problems associated with their sex and generative organs.

Sulphate of Lime (Calc Sulph.) is the tissue salt associated with Scorpio. Its action helps to eliminate organic waste products from the body. Cuts are slow to heal when this particular tissue salt is not being assimilated. A deficiency of it can also lead to constipation. Suphate of Lime is naturally found in garlic, which can be added in supplement form to the feed, or in its natural form can be peeled and infused in the water you use to mix the feeds.

PISCES

'This seems serious', said Pooh.
'I must have an escape'.
   Winnie-the-Pooh. A. A. Milne.

~rosehip ~ nettle ~garlic~

raspberry ~ kelp ~ horseradish ~ chicory

~garlic~nettle ~ rosehip~

raspberry ~ kelp ~ horseradish ~ chicory

The gestation time for a mare is approximately ten months. The natural season for covering mares is between the end of February and the beginning of August. Mares covered in the middle of the season will give birth to their foals while the Sun is in the sign of Pisces. The Moon is in Pisces for approximately two and a half days every month. It is therefore quite likely that if your horse or pony was born in the northern hemisphere, Pisces will be either his Sun or his Moon sign.

Probably the most sensitive and vulnerable sign of the zodiac, Pisces, the third water sign is symbolised by the fishes. Just as the fish has no way of protecting itself from danger other than to swim away from it, so your Pisces horse or pony will want to run away when he feels under threat.

Should you wander into a field of horses where one is just standing gazing into the distance, this one is likely to be the Pisces in the herd. When you call him he probably won't hear you. Should you try to entice him with food, it probably won't work. The mundane world is of much less interest to him than the world of the imagination. Pisces horse needs periods of solitude in order to recover from the demands of every day living. If this is not available to him, he will escape into a dream world in order to find it.

An owner who treats a Pisces horse harshly will soon discover his Houdini instincts. The bill for fence repairs will continue to escalate as he finds ever more ways to escape. Here is an animal who needs to feel closely bonded with his owner. Loneliness and isolation will make him anxious and insecure. Ideally he should be with someone who has time to give him the one-to-one love and attention he requires. When Pisces horse feels secure he will put your needs above his own every time, wanting only to please you. Everyone who meets him will love him. But don't think because he is so kind and gentle that he is a 'pushover'. Routine and boredom are the natural enemies of the Pisces horse. He wants to do things when *he* feels like doing them. This will not always correspond with when *you* want him to do them. As you make chase, you might make a mental note to vary his timetable or to engage his interest before you try to impose your will on him.

Although on the surface of things, your Pisces horse or pony appears to be the calm and gentle soul he mostly is – with Pisces nothing is quite what it seems. Beneath a calm exterior are strong undercurrents of which you should be mindful. He does not carry a warning flag designed to alert you to such dangers, but none the less they are there. Confused? Pisces horse will have you 'sussed'. But until you become familiar with the hidden aspects of his nature you could find him quite difficult to fathom.

Essentially a kind and gentle creature who is eager to serve you as best he can, Pisces horse is also extremely impressionable. So much so, that he will instantly recognise the slightest change of mood or attitude towards him and will reflect it back. Such highly developed intuition makes him acutely aware of everything that is going on around him. Quick to sense fear or aggression he will respond accordingly.

Their receptivity makes Pisces horses natural actors and

actresses, who take on the characteristics of those around them as if they were their own. In herd situations, if they fraternise with badly mannered or poorly behaved animals, they instantly pick up those habits.

Should a Pisces horse or pony feel unsafe or unhappy, his fluid and changeable nature will respond by being extremely difficult and uncooperative, evasive and illusive. All he really wants is plenty of affection and a quiet life. Pisces horses will do their best to stay out of trouble, somehow managing to be somewhere else when the going gets tough.

Pisces horses and ponies are naturally good with children (having an instinctive sensitivity to their needs) and it is unusual for them to ever do anything cruel or spiteful. However, you may already have ascertained from what you have read that Pisces horse is not a 'stuffed horse', but needs a confident and competent owner who will handle him with firmness and kindness. He dislikes boundaries, barriers and limits, but without guidance and structure, he will be all over the place. Firm persuasion should achieve the desired results.

If there is a ballet dancer amongst horses, your Pisces horse or pony is it. Blessed with a natural sense of rhythm, his beautiful movement is no better displayed than in the dressage ring when he is performing to music. This is when he should truly come into his own. At one with the music you and he should flow through the test with grace and ease.

Any discipline where the Pisces horse is allowed to show off his natural sense of rhythm and timing will suit him very well. His kind and sensitive temperament makes him an ideal riding school horse and should he be used for trekking he will look after his riders just as well. His gentle Pisces nature makes him the ideal novice ride.

The flexible aspect of Pisces' temperament enables these horses to adapt well to changes in their environment. A home close to water where they can be at one with nature is ideal, but as this is rarely possible, as natural an environment as possible is a good compromise. They are generally happiest when they can be turned out. If they need to live in, Pisces horses should be hacked out as often as possible and given plenty of rhythmic exercise. The open countryside and the exercise will be relaxing and restorative to them.

If a Pisces horse is subjected to a stressful lifestyle where he feels unhappy and insecure, when all else fails he will escape into illness. His body is the barometer for his emotional state. Because Pisces horses are so sensitive and receptive they should respond well to a 'horse whisper' should this type of treatment be appropriate.

Pisces rules the duodenum, the lymphatic system, the pineal and pituitary glands and the feet. As the saying goes 'no foot, no horse'. It is therefore essential that you take good care of your Pisces horse's or pony's feet. He is more than usually susceptible to corns, cracked hooves, navicular and pedal osteitis than other horses are. Poor trimming and shoeing can lead to incorrect foot balance, which can in turn give rise to more lasting foot problems. A good farrier will spot early signs of things going wrong so it is worth selecting your farrier with care. In spring you will need to be alert to early symptoms of laminitis and, remembering his escapist tendencies. You will need to take the necessary steps to keep your Pisces pony away from too much lush spring grass. Garlic, nettle and rosehip are all supplements that can be helpful in preventing laminitis.

Exercise and massage can both help in preventing lymphatic problems. Lack of movement and exercise can slow down or inhibit the flow of lymph through the lymphatic system, resulting in filled legs. Massage to the muscles and tendons can help to correct this and stimulate the flow of lymph. The glands themselves can also swell due to bacteria or toxins being carried to them in the lymph. Infection can produce swelling and the accumulation of excess fluid can then lead to permanently enlarged limbs, pain and possible ulceration.

Worm burden and stress can both adversely affect the duodenum, leading to colic of the small intestine. A carefully planned and properly maintained worming routine will prevent the former. Colocynthis is the homeopathic remedy recommended for spasmodic colic. It can be administered by hand but should only be given after consultation with a vet who specialises in homeopathy. When the pineal and pituitary glands are not functioning properly, ovulation and lactation become problematic. Raspberry is a feed additive commonly used on studs because it is know to aid parturition in mares and fertility in stallions. The leaves are often fed to mares for two months prior to foaling to improve muscle tone and stimulate good milk yield.

Kelp (seaweed) is of great benefit to the Pisces

temperament. Horseradish is valuable in the treatment of glandular problems. Chicory and fenugreek are both soothing for digestive ailments. They are all available as feed supplements.

Phosphate of Iron (Ferr. Phos.) is the tissue salt which is often deficient in the Pisces type. It is valuable in correcting anaemic conditions and may also improve the strength and elasticity of the blood vessels and arteries. It may be of benefit to include barley in your Pisces horse's diet, as Phosphate of Iron occurs naturally in this grain. Alternatively, it can be administered in pill form.

CHAPTER 6

CASE STUDIES

We have put together some case studies to illustrate
how certain horses' charts 'pan out'.

Dutch Courage and Desert Orchid are familiar
names. During their working lives, both were stars of
their diametrically opposite sports. Oscar is a pony,
Blackie a young horse and Felix a more mature horse.

Dutch Courage : Sun Gemini   Moon Cancer
                 Air/Water
Desert Orchid : Sun Aries   Moon Libra
                 Fire/Air
Blackie :   Sun Cancer   Moon Virgo
                 Water/Earth
Oscar :   Sun Leo   Moon Gemini
                 Fire/Air
Felix :   Sun Aries .   Moon Capricorn
                 Fire/Earth.

Should you wish to find out more about astrology and
how it can help you and your horse, please write to
                 Vicky Maloney,
                 Crawley Grange,
                 North Crawley,
                 Milton Keynes,
                 MK16 9HL

DUTCH COURAGE
Owned by Mrs. Jenny Loriston-Clarke
Born 16 June 1969. Holland
Sun Gemini. Moon Cancer

On 16 June 1969 the Sun was in the sign of Gemini and the Moon was in the sign of Cancer. This blends the elements of Air and Water combining intelligence with sensitivity.

Essentially a highly intelligent and versatile creature, Dutch Courage would have been curious, interested and mentally alert. Quick to learn and easy to distract, he may have been easily excited by external stimuli. This coupled with his insatiable curiosity would have made it difficult for him stay focussed. He therefore needed clear instruction and direction. Without this, his natural inclination would have been to flit from one thing to another. His Gemini Sun sign made him extremely adaptable, while his Cancer Moon added fluidity to his nature. A structured training programme was necessary in order to harness his potential and prevent him from being all over the place. Any lack of clear instruction would have left him confused and uncertain of what was expected of him, leading to a loss of confidence that might have produced nervous and scatty behaviour. An owner who could provide him with constancy, reliability and well defined perimeters would have enhanced his sense of well being.

Friendly, gentle and sociable at heart, Dutch Courage enjoyed outings to events and shows. Although his home emvironment would have been a safe haven for him, his Gemini Sun would have enabled him to easily adapt to new situations and surroundings. So long as his routine was familiar to him, a change of environment provided him with the mental stimulus on which he would have thrived. Boredom was his greatest enemy. Should Dutch Courage's lifestyle have been dull and completely predictable, his inevitable restlessness would have led to trouble. A lack of stimulus and variety might have made retirement difficult for him.

The receptive and sensitive qualities bestowed upon him by his Moon sign suggest that he required firm but kind handling. His impressionable temperament indicates that he could pick up bad habits just as quickly and easily as he learned good ones. Kind, genuine and devoted, he would have been completely attached to his owner, looking to her for his safety and security.

Dutch Courage blossomed because he was able to enjoy a familiar living environment and was given plenty of affection. Without this domestic stability, he would not have done so well, but would have displayed highly strung, nervous behaviour and withdrawn, clinging and possessive qualities. As it was, his water Moon sign, combined with his bright, airy Sun made him extremely perceptive. Dutch Courage had a great spark and enthusiasm for his work, as well as the tenacity to stay with it. His innate receptivity and awareness enabled him to read and respond to voice and touch with the swift, light and nimble movement common to Gemini. Such sensitivity, intelligence and agility suggest that he would have done well in a number of disciplines. The one chosen for him was dressage and at this he excelled.

DESERT ORCHID
Owned by Mr.R.Burridge
Born 11 April 1979 England
Sun Aries. Moon Libra.

On 11 April 1979 the Sun was in the sign of Aries and
the Moon was in the sign of Libra. This blends the elements of Fire and Air, inspiration and intelligence.

    This particular combination of Sun sign and
Moon sign brings together the polarities of Aries and
Libra, action and relaxation, independence and the need
for companionship, competition and compromise,
aggression and passivity, assertion and the desire for a
peaceful existence. The 'me first' attitude of Aries can at
times be rather forceful and brash while the 'after you'
response of Libra is considerate and well mannered.
Desert Orchid will have to balance the one against the
other, being at times pulled in the direction of his fiery
spirit while at other times needing to honour his more
laid back and rational side. Balancing two such opposing
characterisitics is not easy. His owner and trainer would
have been aware of his inclination to swing from one
extreme to the other.

    Desert Orchid is at heart a brave and courageous
horse who is very competitive and who wants to win. A
natural leader, he wants to be ahead of the field but his
impatience and his zest for life can lead to a tendency to
rush headlong into things. Such impulsive behaviour can
at times be just what is needed but at other times it can
lead to accidents. He is headstrong and in this he needs a
rider who knows eactly when to give him his head and

when to hold him back. The influence of the Moon in Libra adds thought to his high energy and enthusiasm, enabling him to employ his intelligence and his brawn in order to get what he wants. At best he can take decisive action based upon an intelligent assessment of the situation. At worse he will vascillate, uncertain of when to go and when to stay. Once he has worked out what it is he needs to do, he has the ability to act with speed and alacrity. A decisive rider who can give clear instructions is therefore a great asset to him.

Although he is essentially independent, he will not like being alone. He needs the companionship of his rider, his trainer and ideally another horse. While he is able to work on his own, should he have to live in isolation he would become very withdrawn and depressed. He needs a friend. He also needs to feel love and valued. To this end he will charm his way into people's affections and will do his best to please. If he feels unloved or undervalued he will become anxious and fretful. Similarly if he is subjected to agressive behaviour or to a hostile environment, he will loose his confidence and will quickly go down hill.

With plenty of encouragement and affection this is a horse who will thrive on action. But he does need encouragement if he is not to become dull and inert. A structured training programme will enable him to direct his high energy towards a goal.

A kind, spirited and adventurous horse he was born to win. He was also born to play fair.

BLACKIE
Owned by Beth Maloney
Born 3 July 1995, The Hague, Netherlands.
Sun Cancer. Moon Virgo.

On 3 July 1995 the Sun was in the sign of Cancer and the
Moon was in the sign of Virgo. This blends the elements of
Water and Earth combining sensitivity with practical ability.

This combination of water and earth makes Blackie
both sensitive and perceptive. His vivid imagination and his
sensitivity to the needs of his rider work in harmony with his
attentive and discriminating mind, enabling him to learn
quickly and to learn well. He is responsive to the commands
of voice and touch which he can translate into practical
behaviour. But in order to feel safe and secure he needs to
know exactly what is expected of him and this requires a
structured routine or training programme as well as clear and
precise instruction. Once he understands what his owner or
rider requires of him, his desire to help and serve coupled
with his sensitive and responsive nature will make him more
than willing to deliver the goods. He wants to be productive
and his Virgo Moon makes him ideally suited to any form of
detailed work, which he will strive hard to get just right.
Dressage should suit him well.

Essentially a protective creature, he will be devoted
to his owner, and will expect her devotion in return.
Familiarity is important to his well being. Changes to his
living situation are likely to upset him for a while as will

changes to his diet. A healthy and well balanced diet is essential to his well being. When he is unhappy his stomach will register his dis-ease. Being turned out in the same field and brought back to the same stable where his food is ready and waiting for him, helps him to feel safe and secure. Although he thrives on plenty of affection he is modest and reserved. He therefore needs plenty encouragement if he is to shine. His acute sensitivity makes him more than usually aware of the feelings and moods of his rider. For this reason he will know when she is out of sorts or lacking in confidence and this will adversely affect his own performance.

His devoted nature will blossom when he feels valued and cared for. Harsh criticism or ridicule will have the reverse effect on him. He therefore needs a sensitive owner who he can trust. Someone who can give him the time and attention he needs. With lots of encouragement he will use his imagination and his perception to serve her with affection and to get things just right for her.

OSCAR
Owned by Mrs. Trisha Badham
Born 3 August 1994. Romford, Essex.
Sun Leo. Moon Gemini.

On 3 August 1994 the Sun was in the sign of Leo and the Moon was in the sign of Gemini. This blends the elements of Fire and Air combining inspiration and intelligence.

A theatrical little pony prone to the occassional

dramatic gesture, Leo and Gemini together make Oscar a child at heart. Full of mischief and fun, his warm, affectionate and sunny disposition makes him extremely loveable. But when he is ignored he can become impossible. He is special and he needs to have this specialness affirmed if he is to thrive. Plenty of attention and praise will bring out the best in him. When he knows he is loved and appreciated he will blossom into the delightful animal he is. However, should he feel unloved he will become very difficult, spiteful and bad tempered, resorting to theatrical behaviour and trickery in order to get you to notice him.

His Gemini intelligence unites with the creative inspiration of Leo to make him extremely clever. He is bright and receptive. He is also very proud and wants to shine. The perfect show pony, he is guaranteed to rise to the occassion of the show ring, loving the opportunity to show off. He also possesses the agility, wit and intelligence to do well in competitions, where he will be only too happy to perform. But leave him in a field for too long and you will see the down side of such a sociable and extrovert temperament.. That is – if he is still in the field when you return to him. Fences will not hold him in. He is a real Houdini and will wriggle out of any situation where he feels bored, hemmed in and confined, getting into all kinds of mischief along the way. Keeping Oscar stabled for too long will depress him. When he is down hearted and fretful, he is likely to loose weight and condition very quickly. Under stress his back will also tense and suffer from strain. It is therefore best to keep him busy.

Oscar will be happiest in a home environment where he is given lots of attention and where he will be rewarded for his efforts with plenty of affection, praise and applause.

If he is well cared for, his youthful spirit will stay with him all his life so that he will continue to please and delight the children who look after him, well into old age.

FELIX
Owned by Beth Maloney
Born 19 April 1987, Copenhagen, Denmark.
Sun Aries. Moon Capricorn

On 19 April 1987, the Sun was in the sign of Aries and the Moon was in the sign of Capricorn, blending the elements of Fire and Earth - inspiration and practical ability.

When the signs of Aries and Capricorn unite in this way, life is likely to be a challenge. Essentially an energetic, enthusiastic and independent creature who wants to be given his head, Felix responds to new situations with sensitivity and caution. An 'action man', the fire of Aries inspires him to take the initiative and lead the field. He is very competitive and wants to win. But if he feels apprehensive or insecure, doubts and uncertainties will hold him back. He therefore needs to be given lots of encouragement and confident handling. Once Felix gets going, he is likely to be unstoppable. His rider will therefore need to know exactly how and when to apply the brakes. The persistence of his Capricorn Moon sign combines with the ardent enthusiasm of his Aries Sun sign to make him extremely determined and persistent. Given that he is also very strong, a battle of brawn is not advisable. He wants to be the boss. Anticipating his needs can avoid confrontation. Firm but kind handling using wit and intelligence to persuade him, rather than force to bully him is likely to produce the best results. This is because Felix is sensitive to criticism. Harsh words will have a profound affect upon him. He wants the approval of his owner and rider. To this end he will work hard to achieve their goals for him. However, should he feel he has failed he will become very withdrawn and anxious, losing weight and condition. Praise and encouragement are therefore important to his well being.

The fire at the heart of Felix gives him an abundance of energy that needs to be channelled into work. Otherwise he could become lazy and aggressive. When he is not given sufficient exercise he will also put on too much weight. For this reason his diet should be carefully blanced against the work he is doing. Should he be kept in a sedentary lifestyle without balancing his diet accordingly he will soon begin to resemble an elephant or a hippopotamus.

There is a childlike quality to Felix's temperament which is endearing and refreshing. He can also be quite self controlled. More well suited to work that combines structure with speed, he learns quickly and well, possessing the qualities it takes to be successful in the discipline chosen for him.

A home environment where he is given a structured training programme with plenty of activity and an opportunity to let off steam will be ideal for him.

THE CHARTS

Sun sign and Moon sign

Tables

1985 - 2010

SUN SIGN TABLES FOR 1985 – 1999

Year	85	86	87	88	89	90	91	92	93	94	95	96	97
Jan	21 ♒︎	21 ♒︎	21 ♒︎	21 ♒︎	21 ♒︎	21 ♒︎	21 ♒︎	21 ♒︎	21 ♒︎	21 ♒︎	21 ♒︎	21 ♒︎	21 ♒︎
Feb	19 ♓︎	19 ♓︎	20 ♓︎	20 ♓︎	19 ♓︎	19 ♓︎	20 ♓︎	20 ♓︎	19 ♓︎	19 ♓︎	20 ♓︎	20 ♓︎	19 ♓︎
Mar	21 ♈︎	21 ♈︎	22 ♈︎	21 ♈︎	21 ♈︎	21 ♈︎	22 ♈︎	21 ♈︎	21 ♈︎	21 ♈︎	22 ♈︎	21 ♈︎	21 ♈︎
Apr	21 ♉︎	21 ♉︎	21 ♉︎	20 ♉︎	21 ♉︎	21 ♉︎	21 ♉︎	20 ♉︎	21 ♉︎	21 ♉︎	21 ♉︎	20 ♉︎	21 ♉︎
May	22 ♊︎	22 ♊︎	22 ♊︎	21 ♊︎	22 ♊︎	22 ♊︎	22 ♊︎	21 ♊︎	22 ♊︎	22 ♊︎	22 ♊︎	21 ♊︎	22 ♊︎
Jun	22 ♋︎	22 ♋︎	22 ♋︎	22 ♋︎	22 ♋︎	22 ♋︎	22 ♋︎	22 ♋︎	22 ♋︎	22 ♋︎	22 ♋︎	22 ♋︎	22 ♋︎
Jul	23 ♌︎	24 ♌︎	24 ♌︎	23 ♌︎	23 ♌︎	24 ♌︎	24 ♌︎	23 ♌︎	23 ♌︎	24 ♌︎	24 ♌︎	23 ♌︎	23 ♌︎
Aug	24 ♍︎	24 ♍︎	24 ♍︎	23 ♍︎	24 ♍︎	24 ♍︎	24 ♍︎	23 ♍︎	24 ♍︎	24 ♍︎	24 ♍︎	23 ♍︎	24 ♍︎
Sept	24 ♎︎	24 ♎︎	24 ♎︎	23 ♎︎	24 ♎︎	24 ♎︎	24 ♎︎	23 ♎︎	24 ♎︎	24 ♎︎	24 ♎︎	23 ♎︎	24 ♎︎
Oct	24 ♏︎	24 ♏︎	24 ♏︎	24 ♏︎	24 ♏︎	24 ♏︎	24 ♏︎	24 ♏︎	24 ♏︎	24 ♏︎	24 ♏︎	24 ♏︎	24 ♏︎
Nov	23 ♐︎	23 ♐︎	23 ♐︎	23 ♐︎	23 ♐︎	23 ♐︎	23 ♐︎	23 ♐︎	23 ♐︎	23 ♐︎	23 ♐︎	23 ♐︎	23 ♐︎
Dec	22 ♑︎	23 ♑︎	23 ♑︎	22 ♑︎	22 ♑︎	23 ♑︎	23 ♑︎	22 ♑︎	22 ♑︎	23 ♑︎	23 ♑︎	22 ♑︎	22 ♑︎

SUN SIGN TABLES FOR 1999 – 2010

Year	98	99	00	01	02	03	04	05	06	07	08	09	10
Jan	21 ♒	21 ♒	21 ♒	21 ♒	21 ♒	21 ♒	21 ♒	20 ♒	21 ♒	21 ♒	21 ♒	20 ♒	21 ♒
Feb	19 ♓	20 ♓	20 ♓	19 ♓	19 ♓	20 ♓	20 ♓	19 ♓	19 ♓	20 ♓	20 ♓	19 ♓	19 ♓
Mar	21 ♈	22 ♈	21 ♈	21 ♈	22 ♈	21 ♈	21 ♈	21 ♈	22 ♈	21 ♈	21 ♈	21 ♈	22 ♈
Apr	21 ♉	21 ♉	20 ♉	21 ♉	21 ♉	21 ♉	20 ♉	20 ♉	21 ♉	21 ♉	20 ♉	20 ♉	21 ♉
May	22 ♊	22 ♊	21 ♊	21 ♊	22 ♊	22 ♊	21 ♊	21 ♊	22 ♊	22 ♊	21 ♊	21 ♊	22 ♊
Jun	22 ♋	22 ♋	22 ♋	22 ♋	22 ♋	22 ♋	22 ♋	22 ♋	22 ♋	22 ♋	22 ♋	22 ♋	22 ♋
Jul	24 ♌	24 ♌	23 ♌	23 ♌	24 ♌	24 ♌	23 ♌	23 ♌	23 ♌	24 ♌	23 ♌	23 ♌	23 ♌
Aug	24 ♍	24 ♍	23 ♍	24 ♍	24 ♍	24 ♍	23 ♍	24 ♍	24 ♍	24 ♍	23 ♍	23 ♍	24 ♍
Sept	24 ♎	24 ♎	23 ♎	23 ♎	24 ♎	24 ♎	23 ♎	23 ♎	24 ♎	24 ♎	23 ♎	23 ♎	24 ♎
Oct	24 ♏	24 ♏	24 ♏	24 ♏	24 ♏	24 ♏	24 ♏	24 ♏	24 ♏	24 ♏	24 ♏	24 ♏	24 ♏
Nov	23 ♐	23 ♐	23 ♐	23 ♐	23 ♐	23 ♐	23 ♐	23 ♐	23 ♐	23 ♐	23 ♐	23 ♐	23 ♐
Dec	23 ♑	23 ♑	22 ♑	22 ♑	23 ♑	23 ♑	22 ♑	22 ♑	23 ♑	23 ♑	22 ♑	22 ♑	22 ♑

Moon Sign Table for 1985

1985	Jan	Feb	Ma	Ap	Ma	Jun	Jul	Au	Sep	Oct	No	Dec
1	♈	♊	♊	♌	♍	♏	♐	♒	♓	♈	♊	♋
2	♉		♋		♎		♑		♈	♉		
3		♋		♍		♐		♓			♋	♌
4	♊		♌		♏		♒		♉	♊		
5		♌		♎		♑		♈			♌	♍
6	♋		♍		♐							
7		♍		♏		♒	♓		♊	♋		♎
8			♎		♑			♉			♍	
9	♌	♎		♐		♓	♈		♋	♌		♏
10			♏					♊		♎		
11	♍	♏			♑	♒				♍		♐
12						♈	♉		♌	♏		
13	♎	♐	♐	♒	♓			♋		♎		♑
14						♉	♊		♍		♐	
15	♏		♑		♈			♌		♏		♒
16		♑		♓					♎		♑	
17	♐		♒			♊	♋	♍		♐		♓
18		♒		♈	♉				♏		♒	
19	♑		♓			♋	♌	♎		♑		
20		♓							♐		♓	♈
21				♉	♊		♍					
22	♒		♈			♌		♏	♑	♒		♉
23		♈		♊	♋		♎				♈	
24	♓		♉			♍		♐	♒	♓		
25		♉			♌		♏				♉	♊
26	♈			♋		♎		♑		♈		
27			♊				♐		♓			♋
28	♉	♊		♌	♍	♏		♒		♉	♊	
29			♋						♈			
30			♍	♎	♐	♑	♓				♋	♌
31	♊									♊		

Moon Sign Table for 1986

86	Jan	Feb	Ma	Ap	Ma	Jun	Jul	Au	Sep	Oct	No	Dec
1	♍	♎	♏	♑	♒	♓	♉	♊	♋	♍	♎	♏
2		♏				♈			♌		♏	♐
3	♎				♓		♋					
4				♒		♊			♍	♎	♐	♑
5			♑	♈				♌				
6	♏	♑		♓			♋		♎	♏	♑	♒
7		♒				♊						
8		♒		♈	♉		♍	♏	♐		♒	♓
9						♋	♌					
10	♑	♓	♓		♊		♎				♓	♈
11				♉			♍	♐				
12	♒	♈	♈			♌		♏			♒	♉
13				♊	♋				♑		♈	
14	♓	♉	♉			♍	♎	♐		♓		
15					♌				♒		♉	♊
16	♈			♋		♎	♏	♑		♈		
17		♊	♊							♓		♋
18				♌	♍		♐	♒			♊	
19	♉		♋			♏				♉		
20		♋			♎		♑		♈		♋	♌
21	♊			♍		♐	♓			♊		
22		♌	♌		♏		♒		♉			♍
23			♎			♑		♈			♌	
24	♋	♍	♍		♐		♓			♋		
25				♏		♒		♉	♊		♍	♎
26	♌	♎	♎		♑			♈		♌		
27				♐		♓			♋		♎	♏
28	♍		♏		♒			♊				
29				♑		♈	♉			♍		♐
30			♐		♓			♋	♌		♏	
31	♎						♊			♎		♑

Moon Sign Table for 1987

'87	Jan	Feb	Ma	Ap	Ma	Jun	Jul	Au	Sep	Oct	No	Dec
1	♑	♓	♓	♉	♊	♋	♍	♎	♐	♑	♓	♈
2	♒		♈			♌						
3		♈		♊	♋			♏	♑	♒	♈	♉
4	♓		♉			♍	♎					
5		♉		♋	♌			♐	♒	♓	♉	♊
6	♈						♏					
7		♊	♊			♎		♑	♓	♈		♋
8				♌	♍		♐				♊	
9	♉		♋			♏		♒	♈	♉		♌
10		♋		♍	♎		♑			♋		
11	♊					♐		♓	♉	♊		
12		♌	♌		♏		♒				♌	♍
13				♎		♑		♈				
14	♋		♍				♓		♊	♋		
15		♍		♏	♐	♒		♉			♍	♎
16	♌		♎						♋	♌		
17		♎			♐	♑	♓	♈	♊		♎	♏
18												
19	♍		♏	♑	♒	♈	♉		♌	♍		♐
20		♏						♋			♏	
21	♎		♐	♒	♓		♊	♍	♎			♑
22		♐				♉		♌		♐		
23	♏		♑		♈				♏			
24		♑		♓		♊	♋	♎		♑		
25	♐		♒		♉		♍					♓
26	♒			♈		♋	♌	♏	♐		♒	
27	♑		♓					♎				
28		♓		♉	♊				♐	♑	♓	♈
29	♒		♈			♌	♍					
30				♊	♋			♏	♑	♒	♈	♉
31	♓						♎					

Moon Sign Table for 1988

'88	Jan	Feb	Ma	Ap	Ma	Jun	Jul	Au	Sep	Oct	No	Dec
1	♊	♋	♌	♍	♎	♐	♑	♓	♉	♊	♌	♍
2		♌		♎	♏	♑	♒	♈		♋		
3			♍						♊			
4	♋			♏	♐	♒	♓	♉			♍	♎
5									♋	♌		
6	♌		♎			♑		♈			♎	♏
7		♎		♐		♓		♊	♍			
8			♏		♒		♉		♌			♐
9				♑		♈		♋		♏		
10		♏	♐		♓		♊		♍	♎		
11	♎			♒		♉		♌			♐	♑
12				♈						♏		
13	♏	♐	♑	♓		♊	♋		♎		♑	♒
14		♑						♍				
15			♒		♉	♋	♌		♏	♐		♓
16		♒						♎			♒	
17	♐		♓	♉	♊				♑			♈
18	♑	♓				♌	♍		♐		♓	
19			♈	♊	♋			♏		♒		♉
20	♒	♈				♍	♎		♑		♈	
21			♉		♌			♐		♓		♊
22	♓	♉		♋					♒		♉	
23			♊			♎	♏					
24	♈		♌	♋	♍			♑	♓	♈	♊	♋
25		♊	♋			♏	♐					
26	♉				♎			♒	♈	♉	♋	♌
27		♋		♍			♑					
28	♊		♌			♐		♓	♉	♊		♍
29			♎	♏			♒			♌		
30			♍			♑		♈	♊	♋		
31	♋				♐		♓					♎

Moon Sign Table for 1989

'89	Jan	Feb	Ma	Ap	Ma	Jun	Jul	Au	Sep	Oct	No	Dec
1	♎	♐	♐	♒	♓	♉	♊	♌	♍	♎	♐	♑
2	♏									♏		
3		♑	♑		♈	♊	♋		♎			♒
4				♓				♍			♑	
5	♐		♒		♉		♌			♐		
6		♒		♈		♋		♎	♏		♒	♓
7	♑			♓			♍			♑		
8		♓		♉		♌			♐		♓	♈
9	♒		♈		♋			♏				
10		♈		♊		♍	♎		♑	♒	♈	♉
11	♓		♉		♌			♐				
12		♉		♋			♏		♒	♓	♉	♊
13	♈		♊			♎						
14		♊		♌	♍			♑	♓	♈	♊	♋
15	♉		♋			♏	♐					
16		♋		♍	♎			♒	♈	♉	♋	♌
17							♑					
18	♊		♌			♐		♓	♉	♊		♍
19		♌		♎	♏						♌	
20	♋		♍			♑	♒	♈		♋		
21		♍			♐						♍	♎
22	♌			♏		♒	♓	♉	♊	♌		
23			♎								♎	♏
24		♎		♐	♑	♓	♈		♋			
25	♍		♏					♊		♍		
26		♏		♑	♒		♉		♌		♏	♐
27	♎					♈		♋		♎		
28			♐	♒	♓				♍		♐	♑
29						♉		♌				
30	♏		♑		♈		♋		♎	♏		♒
31								♍				

Moon Sign Table for 1990

'90	Jan	Feb	Ma	Ap	Ma	Jun	Jul	Au	Sep	Oct	No	Dec
1	♒	♈	♈	♊	♋	♍	♎	♐	♑	♒	♈	♉
2	♓	♉	♉	♋	♌	♎	♏		♒	♓		♊
3											♉	
4	♈	♊	♊	♌	♍			♑		♈		♋
5						♏	♐		♓		♊	
6	♉		♋		♎			♒		♉		♌
7		♋		♍		♐	♑		♈		♋	
8	♊		♌					♓		♊		♍
9		♌		♎	♏				♉		♌	
10	♋		♍			♑	♒			♋		
11		♍		♏	♐			♈	♊		♍	♎
12	♌					♒	♓					
13		♎	♎					♉	♋	♌	♎	♏
14				♐	♑		♈					
15	♍		♏			♓		♊	♌	♍		
16		♏			♒		♉				♏	♐
17	♎			♑				♋		♎		
18		♐	♐						♍		♐	♑
19				♒	♓	♉	♊	♌				
20	♏		♑						♎	♏		
21		♑		♓	♈	♊	♋	♍			♑	♒
22	♐								♏	♐		
23		♒	♒	♈	♉	♋	♌				♒	♓
24	♑						♎					
25		♓	♓	♉	♊	♌	♍		♐	♑		♈
26								♏			♓	
27	♒		♈	♊	♋	♍	♎		♑	♒		
28		♈						♐			♈	♉
29	♓		♉	♋	♌					♓		
30						♎	♏		♒		♉	♊
31	♈		♊		♍			♑				

Moon Sign Table for 1991

'91	Jan	Feb	Ma	Ap	Ma	Jun	Jul	Au	Sep	Oct	No	Dec
1	♋	♍	♍	♏	♐	♑	♒	♈	♉	♋	♍	♎
2						♒	♓		♊			
3	♌							♉		♌		♏
4				♐	♑				♋		♎	
5	♍		♏			♓	♈	♊		♍		
6		♏		♑	♒			♌			♏	♐
7			♐			♈	♉	♋		♎		
8	♐								♍		♐	♑
9	♏			♒	♓		♊	♌				
10			♑			♉			♎	♏		
11		♑		♓	♈		♋	♍			♑	♒
12	♐					♊		♏	♐			
13		♒	♒				♌				♒	♓
14	♑			♈		♋		♎		♑		
15		♓	♓		♊		♍		♐			
16				♉		♌		♏			♓	♈
17	♒		♈			♋	♎		♑	♒		
18		♈		♊		♍	♏	♐			♈	♉
19	♓		♉							♓		
20		♉		♋		♎			♒		♉	♊
21			♊		♍		♐	♑				
22	♈	♊		♌		♏			♓	♈		♋
23							♑	♒			♊	
24	♉	♋	♋	♍	♎				♈	♉		♌
25						♐v				♋		
26	♊	♌	♌	♎	♏		♒	♓			♊	♍
27						♑			♉	♌		
28	♋		♍				♓	♈		♋		♎
29				♏	♐				♊		♍	
30	♌		♎			♒		♉		♌		♏
31					♑							

Moon Sign Table for 1992

'92	Jan	Feb	Ma	Ap	Ma	Jun	Jul	Au	Sep	Oct	No	Dec
1	♏	♑	♒	♓	♈	♊	♋	♍	♏	♐	♑	♒
2	♐				♉		♌				♒	♓
3		♒		♈		♋		♎		♑		
4			♓				♍		♐			♈
5				♉	♊	♌		♏			♓	
6		♓	♈						♑	♒		
7	♒			♊		♍	♎	♐			♈	♉
8		♈								♓		
9	♓		♉	♋	♌	♎	♏		♒		♉	♊
10		♉						♑				
11			♊		♍	♏			♓	♈		♋
12	♈			♌							♊	
13		♊	♋		♎	♐	♑		♈	♉		♌
14	♉			♍							♋	
15		♋	♌		♏			♓				
16	♊			♎		♑	♒		♉	♊	♌	♍
17		♌	♍		♐			♈				
18	♋			♏		♒	♓		♊	♋	♍	♎
19		♍	♎									
20	♌			♐	♑			♉		♌	♎	♏
21		♎	♏			♓	♈		♋			
22	♍			♑	♒			♊		♍		♐
23		♏					♉		♌		♏	
24	♎					♈		♋		♎		♑
25		♐		♒	♓				♍		♐	
26						♉	♊	♌		♏		
27	♏				♈				♎		♑	♒
28		♑		♓		♊	♋	♍		♐		
29	♐		♒						♏		♒	♓
30				♈	♉	♋	♌					
31			♓							♑		

Moon Sign Table for 1993

'93	Jan	Feb	Ma	Ap	Ma	Jun	Jul	Au	Sep	Oct	No	Dec
1	♈	♉	♊	♋	♍	♎	♐	♑	♓	♈	♉	♊
2		♊				♏		♒			♊	♋
3	♉								♈	♉		
4		♋	♋	♍	♎	♐	♑				♋	♌
5								♓				
6	♊	♌	♌	♎	♏	♑	♒		♉	♊		♍
7								♈			♌	
8	♋	♍	♍	♏	♐		♓		♊	♋		♎
9						♒					♍	
10	♌	♎	♎	♐	♑			♉		♌		♏
11						♓	♈		♋		♎	
12	♍	♏	♏	♑	♒		♊					♐
13						♈	♉		♌	♍	♏	
14	♎		♐					♋				
15		♐		♒	♓				♍	♎	♐	♑
16	♏		♑			♉	♊					
17		♑		♓	♈			♌	♎	♏	♑	♒
18	♐					♊	♋					
19		♒	♒					♍	♏	♐	♒	♓
20				♈	♉		♌					
21	♑		♓			♋		♎	♐	♑		
22		♓		♉	♊		♍				♓	♈
23	♒					♌		♏	♑	♒		
24		♈	♈		♋		♎				♈	♉
25				♊		♍		♐		♓		
26	♓		♉				♏		♒			
27		♉		♋	♌	♎		♑			♉	♊
28	♈		♊						♓	♈		
29				♌	♍	♏	♐	♒			♊	♋
30										♉		
31	♉		♋		♎		♑					♌

Moon Sign Table for 1994

'94	Jan	Feb	Ma	Ap	Ma	Jun	Jul	Au	Sep	Oct	No	Dec
1	♌	♎	♎	♐	♑	♓	♈	♊	♋	♌	♎	♏
2	♍				♒							
3				♑		♈	♉		♌	♍	♏	♐
4	♎		♐					♋				
5		♐			♓				♍	♎	♐	♑
6			♑			♉	♊					
7		♑		♓	♈			♌	♎	♏	♑	♒
8						♊	♋					
9	♐	♒	♒					♍		♐	♒	♓
10				♈	♉		♌	♏				
11	♑		♓			♋		♎		♑		♈
12		♓		♉	♊						♓	
13	♒		♈			♌	♍	♏		♒		
14		♈							♑		♈	♉
15	♓			♊	♋	♍	♎	♐		♓		
16		♉							♒			♊
17		♉		♋	♌		♏				♉	
18	♈					♎		♑		♈		
19		♊	♊		♍		♐		♓		♊	♋
20	♉			♌	♏			♒		♉		
21			♋	♎		♑			♈			♌
22		♋		♍	♐			♓			♋	
23	♊		♌		♏		♒	♑		♊		
24		♌		♎		♑		♈			♌	♍
25	♋				♐					♋		
26		♍	♍	♏		♒	♓		♊			♎
27					♑			♉			♍	
28	♌	♎	♎	♐		♓	♈			♌		♏
29								♊	♋		♎	
30	♍		♏	♑	♒	♉				♍		♐
31								♌				

Moon Sign Table for 1995

'95	Jan	Feb	Ma	Ap	Ma	Jun	Jul	Au	Sep	Oct	No	Dec
1	♑	♒	♓	♈	♉	♋	♌	♍	♏	♐	♒	♓
2		♓		♉	♊			♎	♐	♑	♓	♈
3	♒		♈			♌	♍					
4		♈						♏	♑	♒	♈	♉
5	♓			♊			♎					
6			♉			♍		♐	♒	♓		♊
7		♉	♊		♌						♉	
8	♈		♊		♎	♏	♑					
9		♊			♍				♓		♊	♋
10	♉			♌		♏	♐	♒		♉		
11									♈			♌
12			♍	♎	♐	♑	♓			♋		
13	♊		♌						♉	♊		
14		♌		♎	♏	♑	♒	♈			♌	♍
15									♊	♋		
16		♍	♍	♏	♐	♒	♓					♎
17								♉			♍	
18	♌		♎	♐	♑	♓	♈		♋	♌		
19		♎						♊			♎	♏
20	♍		♏	♑	♒		♉		♌	♍		
21	♏				♈						♏	♐
22	♎	♐		♓			♋					
23		♐		♒		♉	♊		♍	♎	♐	♑
24	♏		♑	♈			♌					
25		♑		♓			♋		♎	♏	♑	♒
26		♒				♊	♍					
27	♐	♒		♈	♉				♏	♐	♒	♓
28						♋	♌					
29	♑		♓	♉	♊			♎	♐	♑	♓	♈
30							♍					
31	♒		♈					♏		♒		♉

Moon Sign Table for 1996

'96	Jan	Feb	Ma	Ap	Ma	Jun	Jul	Au	Sep	Oct	No	Dec
1	♉	♋	♋	♍	♎	♏	♑	♓	♈	♉	♋	♌
2			♌			♐			♉	♊		
3				♎	♏		♒	♈			♌	♍
4		♌				♑			♊	♋		
5					♐		♓				♍	♎
6				♏		♒		♉				
7			♎			♑	♈		♋	♌		
8	♌	♎			♐			♊			♎	♏
9			♏		♒		♉		♌	♍		
10		♏		♑		♈		♋			♏	♐
11					♓							
12		♐	♐	♒			♊		♍	♎	♐	♑
13	♎					♉		♌				
14		♑	♑	♓	♈		♋		♎	♏		♒
15	♏						♊				♑	
16		♒	♒	♈	♉			♍		♐		♓
17	♐					♋	♌	♏		♒		
18			♓		♊			♎		♑		♈
19	♑	♓		♉			♍		♐		♓	
20			♈			♌		♏		♒		♉
21	♒	♈		♊	♋				♑		♈	
22		♉					♎					
23	♓	♉		♋	♌	♍		♐	♒	♓	♉	♊
24							♏					
25	♈	♊	♊			♎		♑	♓	♈	♊	♋
26				♌	♍		♐					
27	♉		♋			♏		♒	♈	♉		
28		♋		♍	♎		♑				♋	♌
29								♓	♉	♊		
30	♊		♌		♏	♐	♒				♌	♍
31							♈			♋		

Moon Sign Table for 1997

'97	Jan	Feb	Ma	Ap	Ma	Jun	Jul	Au	Sep	Oct	No	Dec
1	♍	♏	♏	♑	♒	♈	♉	♋	♌	♎	♏	♐
2					♓		♊		♍			♑
3				♒		♉		♌				
4	♏		♑		♈				♎	♏	♐	♒
5		♑		♓		♊	♋	♍				
6			♒		♉					♐	♑	
7		♒		♈			♌		♏			♓
8	♑		♓		♊	♋		♎			♒	
9		♓		♉		♌	♍		♐	♑		♈
10	♒		♈					♏			♓	
11		♈		♊	♋					♒		♉
12	♓		♉			♍	♎		♑			
13		♉			♌			♐		♓	♈	♊
14	♈			♋		♎	♏		♒			
15		♊	♊		♍			♑		♈	♉	♋
16				♌					♓			
17	♉					♏	♐	♒		♉	♊	♌
18		♋	♋		♎				♈			
19	♊					♐	♑	♓		♊	♋	
20		♌	♌		♏				♉			♍
21				♎		♑	♒	♈		♋		
22	♋								♊		♌	♎
23		♍	♍	♏	♐	♒	♓	♉				
24	♌								♋	♌	♍	
25		♎	♎	♐	♑		♈	♊				♏
26	♍					♓			♌	♍	♎	
27		♏	♏	♑	♒							♐
28						♈	♉	♋				
29	♎		♐						♍	♎	♏	
30				♒	♓	♉	♊	♌				♑
31	♏				♈					♏		♐

Moon Sign Table for 1998

'98	Jan	Feb	Ma	Ap	Ma	Jun	Jul	Au	Sep	Oct	No	Dec
1	♒	♈	♈	♊	♋	♌	♎	♏	♐	♒	♓	♉
2						♍			♑		♈	
3	♓	♉	♉	♋						♓		♊
4						♎	♏					♋
5	♈		♊	♌				♑				
6		♊			♍	♏			♓	♈		
7	♉		♋	♍				♒		♉		♌
8		♋			♎				♈			
9	♊					♐	♑				♋	
10		♌	♌		♏			♓	♉		♌	♍
11							♒				♌	
12	♋		♍			♑		♈	♊	♋		♎
13		♍			♐		♓				♍	
14	♌		♎			♒		♉	♋	♌		
15		♎			♑		♈				♎	♏
16	♍			♐		♓		♊		♍		
17		♏	♏	♑							♏	♐
18					♒	♈	♉	♋	♌			
19	♎		♐						♍	♎		
20		♐		♒	♓	♉	♊	♌			♐	♑
21	♏								♎	♏		
22		♑	♑	♓		♊	♋				♑	♒
23	♐							♍	♏			
24		♒	♒		♉	♋	♌			♐	♒	♓
25				♈				♎				
26	♑	♓	♓		♊	♌			♐	♑		
27				♉			♍				♓	♈
28	♒	♈	♈		♋			♏				
29				♊		♍	♎		♑	♒	♈	♉
30	♓		♉		♌			♐				
31							♏			♓		♊

Moon Sign Table for 1999

'99	Jan	Feb	Ma	Ap	Ma	Jun	Jul	Au	Sep	Oct	No	Dec
1	♊	♌	♌	♎	♏	♐	♒	♓	♉	♊	♌	♍
2	♋		♍			♑		♈		♋		♎
3		♍		♏	♐				♊		♍	
4			♎			♒	♓	♉		♌		
5		♎			♑				♋		♎	♏
6	♍			♐		♓	♈	♊	♍			
7		♏	♏						♌		♏	♐
8				♑	♒		♉					
9	♎		♐			♈		♋	♍	♎		
10		♐			♓		♊				♐	♑
11	♏		♒			♉		♌	♎	♏		
12		♑	♑	♓	♈		♋				♑	♒
13				♓		♊	♍					
14	♐		♒		♉		♌		♏	♐		
15			♈			♋		♎			♒	♓
16	♑	♒	♓		♊				♐	♑		
17		♓		♉		♌	♍	♏			♓	♈
18	♒				♋							
19		♈	♈	♊			♎		♑	♒		♉
20					♌	♍		♐			♈	
21	♓	♉	♉	♋	♎	♏			♒	♓		♊
22							♑			♉		
23	♈	♊	♊	♌	♍				♓			♋
24						♏	♐			♊		
25	♉	♋	♋	♍	♎			♒	♈		♉	♌
26						♐	♑		♈		♋	
27	♊		♌					♓		♊		♍
28		♌		♎	♏				♉		♌	
29	♋		♍			♑	♒	♈		♋		
30			♏	♐					♊		♍	♎
31	♌		♎			♓				♌		

Moon Sign Table for 2000

'00	Jan	Feb	Ma	Ap	Ma	Jun	Jul	Au	Sep	Oct	No	Dec
1	♏	♐	♑	♒	♓	♉	Ⅱ	♌	♎	♏	♑	♒
2		♑		♓	♈	Ⅱ	♋	♍		♐		
3			♒						♏			
4				♈	♉	♋	♌	♎			♒	♓
5		♒	♓						♐	♑		
6	♑			♉	Ⅱ	♌	♍	♏			♓	♈
7		♓								♒		
8	♒		♈	Ⅱ	♋	♍	♎		♑			♉
9								♐			♈	
10		♈	♉		♌	♎	♏		♒	♓		
11	♓			♋				♑			♉	Ⅱ
12		♉	Ⅱ		♍					♈		
13	♈			♌		♏	♐		♓		Ⅱ	♋
14		Ⅱ	♋		♎			♒				
15				♍		♐	♑		♈	♉	♋	♌
16	♉	♋	♌					♓				
17				♎	♏				♉	Ⅱ	♌	♍
18	Ⅱ	♌				♑	♒					
19			♍	♏	♐			♈		♋	♍	♎
20	♋	♍				♒	♓		Ⅱ			
21			♎					♉		♌		♏
22	♌	♎		♐	♑				♋	♎		
23			♏			♓	♈	Ⅱ		♍		♐
24	♍			♑	♒				♌	♏		
25		♏	♐			♈	♉	♋		♎		
26	♎								♍		♐	♑
27		♐		♒	♓		Ⅱ	♌				
28	♏		♑			♉			♎	♏		♒
29				♓	♈		♋	♍			♑	
30			♒			Ⅱ				♏	♐	
31	♐				♉		♌					♓

Moon Sign Table for 2001

'01	Jan	Feb	Ma	Ap	Ma	Jun	Jul	Au	Sep	Oct	No	Dec
1	♓	♉	♉	♋	♌	♎	♏	♑	♒	♓	♉	♊
2	♈									♈		
3				♌	♍	♏	♐		♓		♊	♋
4								♒				
5	♉		♋	♍	♎	♐	♑		♈	♉		♌
6		♋						♓			♋	
7			♌	♎	♏		♒			♊		♍
8		♌				♑		♉			♌	
9	♋	♍	♍	♏	♐			♈		♋		♎
10						♒	♓			♊	♍	
11	♌	♎	♎	♑				♉				♏
12				♐					♋	♌	♎	
13	♍		♏			♓	♈					
14		♏		♑	♒			♊	♌	♍	♏	♐
15	♎		♐			♈	♉					
16		♐			♓			♋	♍	♎	♐	♑
17	♏			♒			♊					
18		♑	♑			♉		♌	♎	♏		♒
19			♓	♈			♋				♑	
20	♐		♒			♊		♍	♏	♐		
21		♒		♉			♌				♒	♓
22	♑			♈		♋		♎	♐	♑		
23		♓	♓	♊			♍				♓	♈
24				♉		♌		♏				
25	♒		♈				♎		♑	♒		
26		♈		♊	♋	♍		♐			♈	♉
27	♓								♒	♓		
28		♉	♉	♋	♌	♎	♏				♉	♊
29								♑				
30	♈		♊	♌	♍	♏	♐		♓	♈		
31								♒				

Moon Sign Table for 2002

'02	Jan	Feb	Ma	Ap	Ma	Jun	Jul	Au	Sep	Oct	No	Dec
1	♌	♍	♎	♏	♑	♒	♓	♉	♊	♋	♍	♎
2		♎		♐		♓	♈		♋	♌		♏
3	♍		♏								♎	
4		♏		♑	♒					♍		♐
5			♐			♈	♉	♊	♌		♏	
6	♎	♐		♒	♓					♎		♑
7							♊	♋	♍		♐	
8	♏	♑	♑			♉				♏		♒
9				♓	♈				♎		♑	
10	♐		♒			♊	♋	♌				
11		♒		♈	♉				♏	♐	♒	♓
12	♑					♋	♌	♍				
13		♓	♓						♐	♑	♓	♈
14				♉	♊	♌	♍	♎				
15	♒		♈						♑	♒		
16		♈		♊	♋		♎	♏			♈	♉
17	♓					♍			♒	♓		
18		♉	♉		♌			♐				♊
19				♋		♎	♏			♈	♉	
20	♈		♊		♍				♓			♋
21		♊		♌		♏	♐	♑			♊	
22	♉								♈	♉		
23		♋	♋	♍	♎	♐		♒			♋	♌
24												
25	♊	♌	♌	♎	♏	♑			♉	♊		♍
26							♒				♌	
27	♋	♍	♍	♏	♐	♒			♊	♋		♎
28							♓	♈			♍	
29	♌		♎	♐	♑							♏
30						♓	♈		♋	♌	♎	
31	♍		♏		♒			♊				♐

Moon Sign Table for 2003

'03	Jan	Feb	Ma	Ap	Ma	Jun	Jul	Au	Sep	Oct	No	Dec
1	♐	♒	♒	♈	♉	♊	♋	♍	♏	♐	♒	♓
2	♑					♋	♌					
3		♓	♓					♎	♐	♑	♓	♈
4				♉	♊		♍					
5	♒		♈			♌		♏	♑	♒		♉
6		♈		♊	♋						♈	
7	♓					♍	♎	♐		♓		
8		♉	♉						♒		♉	♊
9	♈			♋	♌	♎	♏	♑		♈		
10			♊						♓			
11		♊		♌	♍	♏	♐	♒			♊	♋
12	♉							♈	♉			
13		♋	♋		♎	♐	♑				♋	♌
14	♊			♍				♓		♊		
15			♌		♏	♑	♒		♉			♍
16		♌		♎				♈		♌		
17	♋		♍		♐		♓		♊	♋		
18		♍		♏		♒		♉			♍	♎
19	♌		♎		♑		♈			♌		
20		♎		♐		♓			♋		♎	♏
21	♍		♏		♒			♊				
22		♏		♑		♈	♉		♌	♍	♏	♐
23	♎		♐		♓			♋				
24		♐		♒			♊		♍	♎	♐	♑
25			♑			♉						
26	♏	♑		♓	♈			♌	♎	♏	♑	♒
27						♊	♋					
28	♐	♒	♒		♉			♍	♏	♐	♒	♓
29				♈			♌					
30	♑		♓			♋		♎		♑		♈
31					♊							

Moon Sign Table for 2004

'04	Jan	Feb	Ma	Ap	Ma	Jun	Jul	Au	Sep	Oct	No	Dec
1	♈	♊	♋		♍	♏	♐	♒	♈	♉	♊	♋
2	♉			♍			♑				♋	♌
3		♋			♎	♐		♓		♊		
4	♊		♌				♒		♉			♍
5				♎	♏	♑		♈			♌	
6		♌	♍				♓		♊	♋		
7	♋			♏	♐	♒		♉			♍	♎
8		♍	♎				♈		♋	♌		
9	♌			♐	♑						♎	♏
10		♎				♓		♊				
11			♏	♑	♒	♈	♉		♌	♍		♐
12	♍	♏						♋			♏	
13			♐	♒	♓		♊		♍	♎		♑
14	♎	♐				♉					♐	
15			♑	♓	♈			♌		♏		♒
16	♏					♊	♋		♎		♑	
17		♑	♒		♉			♍		♐		
18	♐			♈			♌		♏		♒	♓
19		♒	♓			♋		♎		♑		♈
20	♑			♉	♊		♍		♐		♓	
21		♓	♈			♌						
22	♒				♋		♎	♏	♑	♒	♈	♉
23		♈		♊		♍						
24	♓		♉				♏	♐	♒	♓		♊
25		♉		♋	♌						♉	
26		♊				♎		♑		♈		
27	♈				♍		♐		♓		♊	♋
28		♊		♌		♏		♒		♉		
29	♉		♋				♑		♈		♋	♌
30				♍	♎	♐						
31			♌					♓		♊		

Moon Sign Table for 2005

'05	Jan	Feb	Ma	Ap	Ma	Jun	Jul	Au	Sep	Oct	No	Dec
1	♍	♎	♏	♐	♒	♓	♉	♊	♌	♍	♎	♐
2		♏		♑		♈		♋			♏	
3	♎		♐		♓		♊		♍	♎		
4		♐		♒		♉					♐	♑
5			♑		♈			♌				
6	♏	♑		♓		♊	♋		♎	♏	♑	♒
7			♒					♍				
8	♐	♒		♈	♉		♌			♐	♒	♓
9						♋						
10	♑	♓	♓	♉	♊			♎		♑		♈
11						♌	♍		♐		♓	
12	♒	♈	♈	♊	♋			♏		♒		♉
13							♎		♑		♈	
14	♓	♉	♉			♍		♐		♓		♊
15				♋	♌						♉	
16	♈		♊			♎	♏	♑		♈		
17		♊		♌	♍				♓		♊	♋
18	♉					♏	♐	♒		♉		
19		♋	♋						♈		♋	♌
20	♊			♍	♎		♑	♓				
21			♌			♐			♉	♊		
22		♌		♎	♏		♒	♈			♌	♍
23	♋					♑			♊	♋		
24		♍	♍		♐		♓				♍	♎
25	♌			♏				♉		♌		
26			♎		♑	♒			♋			
27		♎		♐			♈				♎	♏
28	♍		♏		♒	♓			♌	♍		
29				♑		♈	♉	♋			♏	♐
30	♎		♐		♓					♎		
31							♊					♑

Moon Sign Table for 2006

'06	Jan	Feb	Ma	Ap	Ma	Jun	Jul	Au	Sep	Oct	No	Dec
1	♑	♓	♓	♉	♊	♌	♍	♎	♐	♑	♓	♈
2	♒	♈	♈	♊	♋			♏				
3						♍	♎		♑	♒	♈	♉
4	♓		♉					♐				
5		♉		♋	♌				♒	♓	♉	♊
6	♈		♊			♎	♏					
7		♊		♌	♍			♑	♓	♈	♊	♋
8	♉		♋			♏	♐					
9		♋						♒	♈	♉		♌
10				♍	♎		♑					
11	♊		♌			♐		♓				♍
12		♌		♎	♏		♒				♌	
13	♋		♍			♑		♈		♊	♋	
14		♍			♐		♓				♍	♎
15	♌				♏	♒		♉		♌		
16			♎						♋			♏
17		♎		♐	♑	♓	♈	♊			♎	
18	♍		♏						♌	♍		
19		♏		♑	♒	♈	♉	♋			♏	♐
20	♎									♎		
21			♐		♓	♉	♊		♍			♑
22		♐		♒				♌			♐	
23	♏		♑		♈		♋		♎	♏		♒
24		♑		♓		♊		♍			♑	
25	♐		♒		♉					♐		
26		♒		♈		♋	♌		♏		♒	♓
27	♑		♓		♊			♎				
28		♓		♉		♌	♍		♐	♑	♓	♈
29	♒		♈					♏				
30				♊	♋					♒	♈	♉
31			♉				♎	♐				

Moon Sign Table for 2007

'07	Jan	Feb	Ma	Ap	Ma	Jun	Jul	Au	Sep	Oct	No	Dec
1	♊	♋	♌	♍	♎	♐	♑	♓	♈	♊	♋	♍
2		♌		♎	♏				♉		♌	
3	♋		♍			♑	♒	♈		♋		
4		♍		♏	♐				♊		♍	♎
5	♌					♒	♓	♉		♌		
6			♎						♋		♎	♏
7		♎		♐	♑		♈					
8	♍		♏			♓		♊	♌	♍		
9		♏			♒		♉				♏	♐
10	♎			♑		♈		♋		♎		
11			♐		♓		♊		♍			♑
12		♐		♒		♉		♌			♐	
13	♏		♑				♋		♎	♏		
14		♑		♓	♈	♊		♍			♑	♒
15	♐								♏	♐		
16		♒	♒	♈	♉	♋	♌				♒	♓
17								♎				
18	♑	♓	♓	♉	♊	♌	♍		♐	♑		♈
19								♏			♓	
20	♒	♈	♈	♊	♋		♎		♑	♒		♉
21						♍					♈	
22	♓	♉	♉	♋	♌			♐		♓		♊
23						♎	♏		♒		♉	
24	♈	♊	♊	♌	♍			♑				♋
25							♐		♓	♈	♊	
26	♉		♋			♏		♒				♌
27		♋		♍	♎				♈	♉	♋	
28	♊		♌			♐	♑					
29				♎	♏			♓	♉	♊	♌	♍
30	♋					♑	♒					
31			♍					♈		♋		♎

Moon Sign Table for 2008

'08	Jan	Feb	Ma	Ap	Ma	Jun	Jul	Au	Sep	Oct	No	Dec
1	♎	♐	♐	♒	♓	♉	♊	♌	♍	♎	♐	♑
2			♑						♎	♏		
3	♏	♑		♓	♈	♊	♋	♍			♑	♒
4									♏	♐		
5	♐		♒		♉	♋	♌					♓
6		♒		♈				♎			♒	
7			♓		♊	♌	♍		♐	♑		
8	♑			♉				♏			♓	♈
9		♓	♈		♋		♎		♑	♒		
10	♒			♊		♍		♐			♈	♉
11		♈	♉		♌							
12	♓			♋		♎	♏		♒	♓	♉	♊
13		♉	♊		♍			♑				
14				♌		♏	♐		♓	♈	♊	♋
15	♈	♊	♋					♒				
16				♍	♎				♈	♉	♋	♌
17	♉	♋				♐	♑					
18			♌	♎	♏			♓		♊	♌	♍
19	♊	♌				♑	♒		♉			
20			♍					♈		♋		♎
21	♋			♏	♐				♊		♍	
22		♍	♎			♒	♓	♉		♌		♏
23	♌			♐	♑				♋		♎	
24		♎				♓	♈	♊		♍		
25	♍		♏						♌		♏	♐
26		♏		♑	♒	♉						
27	♎		♐			♈		♋	♍	♎		♑
28				♒	♓		♊				♐	
29		♐				♉		♌	♎	♏		
30	♏		♑		♈		♋				♑	♒
31								♍		♐		

Moon Sign Table for 2009

'09	Jan	Feb	Ma	Ap	Ma	Jun	Jul	Au	Sep	Oct	No	Dec
1	♒	♈	♈	♊	♋	♍	♎	♐	♑	♓	♈	♉
2	♓	♉	♉	♋	♌	♎	♏		♒			♊
3								♑			♉	
4	♈		♊	♌	♍	♏	♐		♓	♈		♋
5		♊						♒			♊	
6	♉		♋	♍	♎					♉		♌
7		♋				♐	♑		♈		♋	
8	♊		♌		♏			♓		♊		♍
9		♌		♎		♑	♒		♉		♌	
10	♋		♍					♈				♎
11		♍		♏	♐				♊	♋	♍	
12	♌		♎			♒	♓					
13		♎		♐	♑			♉	♋	♌	♎	♏
14	♍					♓	♈					
15		♏	♏					♊	♌	♍	♏	♐
16	♎			♑	♒		♉					
17			♐			♈		♋	♍	♎		♑
18		♐		♒	♓						♐	
19	♏		♑			♉	♊	♌		♏		
20		♑			♈				♎		♑	♒
21	♐			♓		♊	♋	♍		♐		
22									♏			♓
23		♒		♈	♉	♋	♌	♎			♒	
24	♑		♓					♐	♐	♑		
25		♓		♉	♊	♌	♍	♏			♓	♈
26	♒								♑	♒		
27		♈	♈	♊	♋	♍	♎					♉
28								♐			♈	
29	♓		♉	♋	♌	♎	♏		♒	♓		
30								♑			♉	♊
31	♈		♊		♍		♐			♈		

Moon Sign Table for 2010

'10	Jan	Feb	Ma	Ap	Ma	Jun	Jul	Au	Sep	Oct	No	Dec
1	♋	♍	♍	♏	♐	♑	♒	♈	♉	♋	♌	♎
2						♒	♓		♊		♍	
3	♌	♎	♎	♐	♑			♉		♌		♏
4						♓	♈		♋	♎		♐
5	♍	♏	♏		♒			♊		♍	♎	♐
6				♑					♌		♏	
7	♎		♐			♈	♉	♋		♎		♑
8		♐		♒	♓				♍		♐	
9	♏		♑			♉	♊	♌		♏		
10		♑			♈					♏	♑	♒
11	♐			♓		♊	♋	♍				
12		♒	♒						♏		♒	♓
13				♈	♉			♎				
14	♑			♓		♋				♐		
15		♓		♉	♊		♍				♓	♈
16	♒					♌		♏	♑	♒		
17			♈		♋		♎				♈	♉
18		♈		♊		♍		♐				
19	♓			♉	♌		♏		♒	♓		
20		♉		♋		♎		♑			♉	♊
21	♈				♍		♐		♓	♈		
22		♊	♊	♌		♏					♊	♋
23								♒				
24	♉	♋	♋	♍	♎	♐	♑		♈	♉		♌
25							♓			♋		
26	♊			♌	♏				♉	♊		♍
27		♌				♑					♌	
28	♋		♍	♏	♐			♈		♋		♎
29						♒	♓		♊		♍	
30	♌			♎	♑			♉				♏
31							♈			♌		

BIBLIOGRAPHY

Aesop's Fables Published by Airmount Publishing
Co.Astrology, Psychology And The Four Elements.
                              ARROYO, M.A., Stephen.
        Published by CRCS Publication
John Betjamin's Collected Poems. BETJEMIN,John
The Marriage of Heaven and Hell BLAKE, William
The Fairy Tale Treasury   BRIGGS and HAVILAND
 Alternative Therapies for Horses. BRITTON,Vanessa.
        Published by Ward Lock.
A Search in Secret Egypt. BRUNTON, Dr. Paul.
        Published by Weiser.
Alice's Adventures in Wonderland   CARROLL,Lewis
Songs from Alice   CARROLL,Lewis
Astrology and Health. GEDDES, D.F. ASTROL. S.,Sheila.
        Published by Aquarian.
The Wind in the Willows   GRAHAM,Kenneth
Veterinary Notes for Horse Owners. HAYES, FRCVS.
Captain M. Horace.
        Published by Prentice Hall Press.
American Ephemiris for the 21st Century at Midnight
                              MICHELSON, Neil,F
        Published by ACS Publications
Winnie the Pooh   MILNE,A.A.
Alan Oken's Complete Astrology. OKEN, Alan.
        Published by Bantam Books Inc.
The Complete Equine Veterinary Manual. PAVORD,
Tony & Marcy.
        Published by David & Charles.

Name: ....

Address:

....

....

....

....

Signature: ....

VISA no: ....

Expiry date:

....

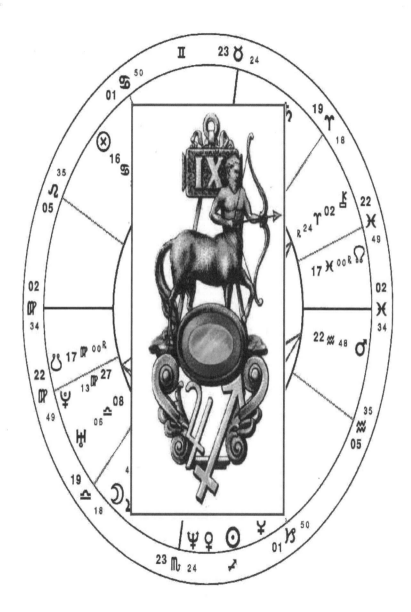